TABLE OF CONTENTS

Unit		Page
	Handwriting Models	2
1	Swift Kick Spellings	3
2	Skate Blade Spellings	8
3	Backhand Compounds	13
4	Pool Crawl Spellings	18
5	Pole-Vault Compounds	23
6	Hurl the Spear Words	28
7	Surfboard Compounds	33
8	Major Hockey Rivals	38
9	Western Athlete Spellings	42
10	Human Comet Words	46
11	Slippery Syllables	50
12	Track Practice Words	55
13	Splendid Defense Words	59
14	Gym Whiz Syllables	64
15	Fosbury Flop Words	68
16	Husky Muscle Syllables	72
17	Spray Waves Syllables	77
18	Speedy Wheels Words	81

Unit		Page
19	Fly High Words	85
20	Polo Solo Syllables	89
21	Super Crew Words	94
22	Rooftop Loop Syllables	99
23	Trout Crowd Syllables	103
24	Poise Pointer Syllables	107
25	Caught the Saucer Words	112
26	Par Star Syllables	116
27	Formal Horse Syllables	121
28	Sturdy Hurdle Words	125
29	Cheer Career Syllables	129
30	Inhale-Exhale Words	133
31	Balance Movement Words	138
32	Unusual Descent Words	142
33	Graceful Opponent Words	146
34	Resistance Excitement Words	150
35	Reluctant Receiver Words	154
36	Elevator Operator Words	158
	Spelling Dictionary	163

HANDWRITING MODELS

a b c d e f g h i

j k l m n o p q r

s t u v w x y z

A B C D E F G H I

J K L M N O P Q R

S T U V W X Y Z

BASIC GOALS IN
SPELLING

SEVENTH EDITION

WILLIAM KOTTMEYER AND AUDREY CLAUS

Webster Division, McGraw-Hill Book Company

New York   St. Louis   San Francisco   Dallas   Atlanta

William Kottmeyer, former Superintendent of the St. Louis Public Schools, is a nationally recognized educational innovator. His spelling and reading publications have received high acclaim for nearly four decades. Dr. Kottmeyer is currently an author-in-residence in the Webster Division.

Audrey Claus is a former teacher and administrator in the St. Louis Public Schools. Miss Claus is co-author of five editions of this spelling series and several reading programs. She, too, is currently an author-in-residence in the Webster Division.

Project Director: Virginia S. Brown
Sponsoring Editor: Richard Paul
Editing Supervisor: Bea Rockstroh
Designers: E. Rohne Rudder and Donna M. Stephens
Production Manager: Tom Goodwin

The photos in this book are by Gary Brady, 13, 17; Warren Bolster/SPORTS ILLUSTRATED, 33, 37; Dr. E.R. Degginger, 95, 98; Phil Degginger, 138, 141; Florida Cypress Gardens, 85, 89; John Henebry, Jr., 46, 49, 59, 63, 99, 102; Frank Oberle, Jr., 4, 9, 25, 30, 35, 42, 43, 45, 50, 54, 77, 80, 103, 106; Lewis Portnoy, 3, 7, 8, 12, 22, 23, 27, 28, 32, 38, 41, 55, 58, 64, 67, 68, 71, 72, 76, 81, 84, 90, 94, 107, 111, 112, 115, 116, 120, 121, 124, 125, 128, 129, 132, 142, 145, 146, 150, 153, 154, 157, 158, 161. Photo research by E. Rohne Rudder.

The illustrations were created by George Ulrich.
The cover design is by E. Rohne Rudder.

The authors are indebted to Scott, Foresman and Company for permission to use and to adapt definitions from the *Thorndike-Barnhart Intermediate Dictionary* and *Thorndike-Barnhart Advanced Dictionary* by E. L. Thorndike and Clarence L. Barnhart. Copyright © 1979 by Scott, Foresman and Company.

1 Swift Kick Spellings

damp
trash
snatch

smell
dent
pledge
flesh

film
thrill
swift
whisk

stock
dodge
knot **H**

tongs
broth

stuck
punch
judge
S sponge

We spell the short-vowel sounds with these vowel letters.

/a/ 🍎 *a* /e/ 🐘 *e* /i/ 🧊 *i*

/o/ 🐙 *o* /ô/ 🦩 *o* /u/ ☂ *u*

1. Write the /a/ and /i/ words. Underline the vowel letter in each word.

_____

_____

2. Write the /e/ and /u/ words, including the snurk.
(A **snurk** is a word with an unexpected spelling.)

_____

_____

3. Write the /o/ and /ô/ words.

_____

These dictionary symbols stand for consonant sounds. /b/ shows the sound that starts **big;** /d/ shows the sound that starts **did;** etc. A sound symbol stands for the same sound, no matter how the sound is spelled.

/b/	big	/n/	not	/ch/	chop
/d/	did	/p/	pin	/sh/	ship
/f/	fat	/r/	run	/th/	thin
/g/	get	/s/	sit	/ŦH/	this
/h/	hat	/t/	top	/hw/	when
/j/	jog	/v/	van	/ng/	sing
/k/	kick	/w/	went	/zh/	measure
/l/	lull	/y/	yes		
/m/	men	/z/	zip		

4. Write the spelling words with these sounds.

    a. /th/   **b.** /sh/   **c.** /ch/

_____

_____

5. Write the spelling words with the /j/ sound.

_____

6. Write the spelling words with the /k/ sound.

_____

1. Write the spelling word that is a plural noun.

Then write the plural forms of 🖼 , 🧽 ,

and ✈ .

_____

2. A **synonym** is a word that means the same or nearly the same as another word. Use words from the spelling list to write the synonyms of these words.

a. wet   **b.** hit   **c.** grab

_____

d. soup   **e.** fast   **f.** junk

_____

3. Write several sentences about what Judge Peg Smith is doing in this drawing. Use at least three spelling words. Use capital letters and periods correctly.

_____

_____

_____

_____

4. Write several sentences about what a boy named Brad is doing in this drawing. Use at least three spelling words. Use capitals and periods correctly.

_____

_____

_____

_____

damp
trash
snatch
smell
dent
pledge
flesh
film
thrill
swift
whisk
stock
dodge
knot
tongs
broth
stuck
punch
judge
sponge

5

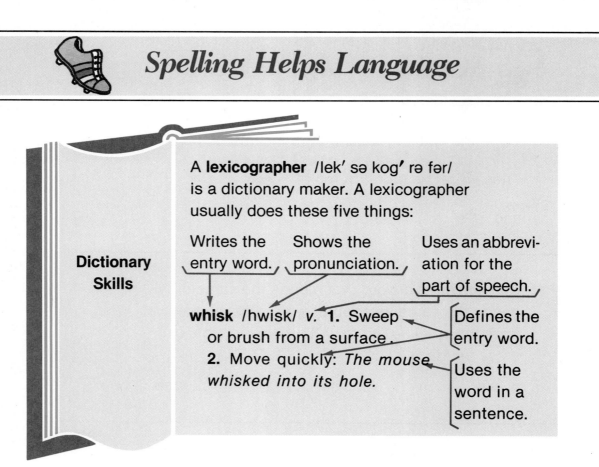

Dictionary Skills

A **lexicographer** /lek′ sə kog′ rə fər/ is a dictionary maker. A lexicographer usually does these five things:

Writes the entry word.

Shows the pronunciation.

Uses an abbreviation for the part of speech.

whisk /hwisk/ *v.* **1.** Sweep or brush from a surface. **2.** Move quickly: *The mouse whisked into its hole.*

Defines the entry word.

Uses the word in a sentence.

1. Do the lexicographer's five jobs for **broth.** Use your own words to write a definition and a sentence. Compare your work with the entry in the Spelling Dictionary.

2. Write **stock, thrill, film,** and **pledge.** After each word, write abbreviations to show the parts of speech.

3. Write **stuck** and the dictionary entry word you find to get the meaning of **stuck.**

Dingle Jingle

If a **quick change** is a "swift shift," what's **insect soup?**

Spelling Helps Reading

Sound out these short-vowel words.

pulp	plunge	glimpse	shrill	dull	peck
weld	melt	clamp	frank	hunt	grudge
hint	golf	patch	lodge	clench	blast

Write the words in each row in the right order. Be ready to give reasons for your answers.

1. sixth   twelfth   tenth   fifth   last
2. tub   cup   pot   flask   vat
3. sprinted   trudged   crept   trotted   jogged
4. leg   neck   hip   chin   chest
5. slap   slug   tap   hit   punch
6. glad   gruff   mad   glum   grim
7. frog   cat   ant   elk   hog
8. socks   pants   belts   vests   hats
9. trim   fat   thin   plump   slim
10. hiss   hum   chant   sing   yell

Look again at the **Swift Kick** picture on page 3. Pretend that you are the player in the green shirt. You score a winning goal with your kick just as the game ends. Write a short report telling about your glorious victory.

Test

2 Skate Blade Spellings

phrase
quail
bray
vane Ⓗ
vain Ⓗ
▽ vein Ⓗ

scheme
creep
feast

quite
spry
blight

clothe
roast
known
mold

dune
cue
juice
hew

Long-vowel sounds have spelling options.

/ā/ ai, ay, a -consonant- e

/ē/ ee, ea, e -consonant- e

/ī/ y, igh, i -consonant- e

/ō/ oa, ow, o(ld), o -consonant- e

/ū/ ue, ui, ew, u -consonant- e

1. Write the /ē/ and /ō/ words. Circle the word with /ŦH/.

2. Write the seven /ū/ and /ī/ words. Underline the word with the /kw/ sounds.

3. Write the six /ā/ words in alphabetical order. Underline the snurk.

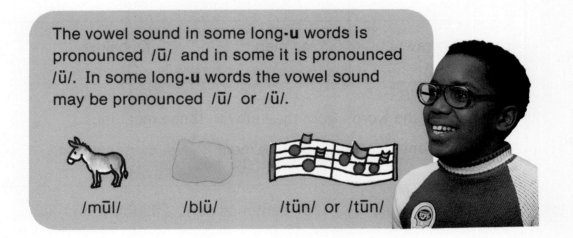

The vowel sound in some long-**u** words is pronounced /ū/ and in some it is pronounced /ü/. In some long-**u** words the vowel sound may be pronounced /ū/ or /ü/.

/mūl/   /blü/   /tün/ or /tūn/

4. Write **dune, due, new, news,** and **suit.** Underline any word you pronounce with /ü/.

Working with the Words

1. Write the words with vowel-consonant-**e** spellings. After each word, write the dictionary sound symbol that shows the vowel sound.

phrase
quail
bray
vane
vain
vein
scheme
creep
feast
quite
spry
blight
clothe
roast
known
mold
dune
cue
juice
hew

2. Write the words with these sounds and spellings.
   Underline the word meaning "put clothes on."

   a. ph = /f/   **b.** f = /f/   **c.** s = /z/

   _____

   d. c = /s/   **e.** th = /ŦH/   **f.** ch = /k/

   _____

3. Write a synonym from the list for each word.
   Underline the two /ū/ words.

   a. chop   **b.** hint   **c.** form

   _____

   d. crawl   **e.** plan   **f.** bake

   _____

4. Write the words from the list with these meanings.

   a. plant disease   **b.** fine meal   **c.** game bird

   _____

   d. donkey's cry   **e.** sentence part   **f.** too proud

   _____

5. Write a sentence or two about Dwight's great-grandmother who is eighty-nine years old. She is quick-moving and says that she is a very proud person who likes colorful dresses. Try to use four spelling words. Proofread your work.

   _____

   _____

Look again at the picture on page 8. What are the two kinds of ice-skating contests? What is meant by "school figures" in skating contests? What is "free skating"? Write a paragraph to answer these questions.

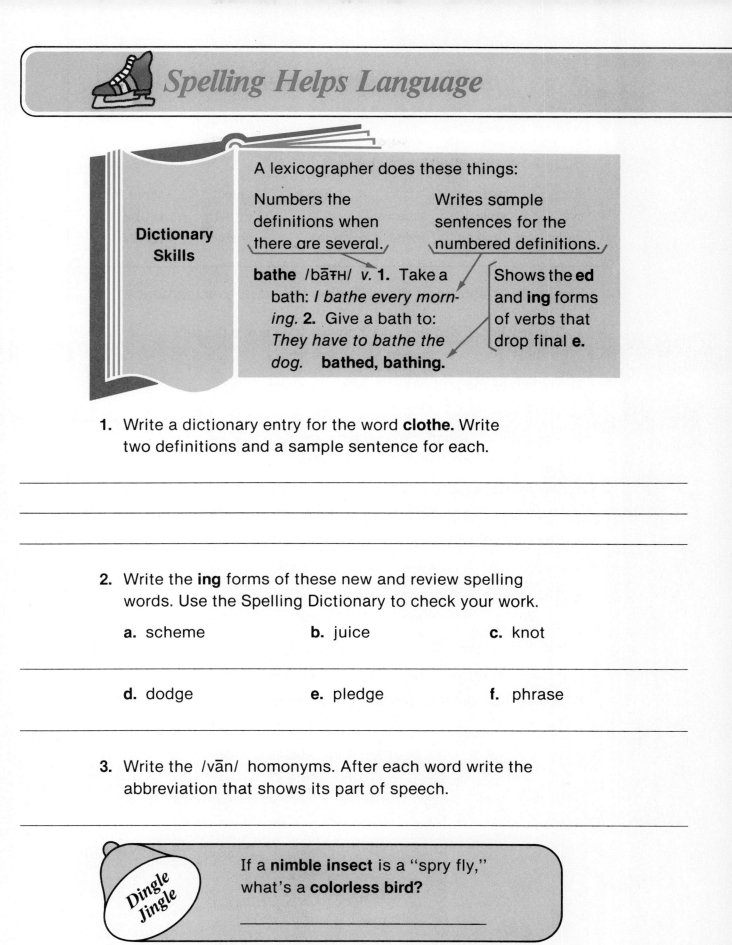

Spelling Helps Language

Dictionary Skills

A lexicographer does these things:

Numbers the definitions when there are several.

Writes sample sentences for the numbered definitions.

bathe /bāᵮH/ *v.* **1.** Take a bath: *I bathe every morning.* **2.** Give a bath to: *They have to bathe the dog.* **bathed, bathing.**

Shows the **ed** and **ing** forms of verbs that drop final **e.**

1. Write a dictionary entry for the word **clothe.** Write two definitions and a sample sentence for each.

_____

_____

_____

2. Write the **ing** forms of these new and review spelling words. Use the Spelling Dictionary to check your work.

   a. scheme   **b.** juice   **c.** knot

   d. dodge   **e.** pledge   **f.** phrase

3. Write the /vān/ homonyms. After each word write the abbreviation that shows its part of speech.

_____

Dingle Jingle

If a **nimble insect** is a "spry fly," what's a **colorless bird?**

_____

11

Sound out these long-vowel words.

spray	prune	strain	screech	glue	scold
eve	style	crease	flight	growth	bruise
oath	quake	spine	quote	chew	raise

Guess the meaning of the underlined word in each sentence.

1. The teacher <u>chided</u> the lad kindly when he broke the rule.

    beat   quoted   scolded   shocked

2. We helped the <u>frail</u> old man cross the street.

    spry   sweet   cold   weak

3. The painter's smock <u>reeks</u> with the smell of stale paint.

    shines   feels   stinks   smokes

4. We do not <u>deem</u> him to be the right one for the job.

    pay   hire   hope   think

5. The silly tale of finding a gold mine was a huge <u>hoax</u>.

    joke   oath   nice find   sly bribe

6. The rain made the streets <u>gleam</u> in the dim light.

    slide   shine   freeze   blue

7. The <u>peal</u> of the bells woke us from our nap.

    groaning   ringing   humming   waving

8. A <u>gale</u> filled the sails and sent our boat speeding away.

    breeze   wave   foam   strong wind

Test

12

3 Backhand Compounds

We spell the parts of compound words with the same short-vowel and long-vowel spelling options you reviewed in Units 1 and 2. Find every option in the **Backhand Compounds.**

handcuff
drumstick
bluegrass
backbone
mainland
nickname
fruitcake
stagecoach
lowland
standby
newsstand
salesmen
peanut
highlight
fireplace
beehive
driveway
yuletide
stronghold
headache

1. Write the compounds with two short-vowel sounds.
   Circle the word that can be used as a verb.

hand cuff

drum stick

blue grass

back bone

main land

nick name

fruit cake

stage coach

low land

stand by

news stand

sales men

pea nut

high light

fire place

bee hive

drive way

yule tide

strong hold

head ache

2. Write the compounds in which vowel-consonant-**e**
spells a long-vowel sound.

_____

_____

_____

3. Write the compound in which **ea** spells /ē/ and
the compound in which **ai** spells /ā/.

_____

4. Write the compounds with two long-vowel sounds.

_____

_____

5. Write the compounds with these sounds and spellings.

   a. y = /ī/   **b. igh** = /ī/   **c. ow** = /ō/

_____

   d. o (ld) = /ō/ **e. ue** = /ü/   **f. ew** = /ū/ or /ü/

_____

6. Write the snurk. Underline the two vowel letters

   that spell /e/. _____

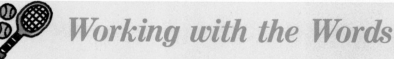

Working with the Words

1. Write the plural form of each pictured noun.

a.   b.   c.

_____

d.   e.   f.

_____

2. Write a synonym from the spelling list for each word or phrase. Underline the word that may be used both as a noun and as a verb.

   a. spine   **b.** fort   **c.** make bright

---

3. Join words from Box A with words from Box B to form nine compounds from the spelling list.

A. nick	news	bee		**B.** by	grass	ache
head	stand	blue		bone	cuff	land
low	back	hand		name	stand	hive

---

4. Join words from Box A with words from Box B to form nine new compounds. Underline the compound that means "a straight line."

A. high	head	bee		**B.** shake	line	plug
fire	stand	land		reel	way	scape
news	blue	hand		still	line	jay

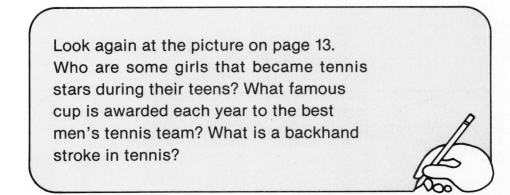

Look again at the picture on page 13. Who are some girls that became tennis stars during their teens? What famous cup is awarded each year to the best men's tennis team? What is a backhand stroke in tennis?

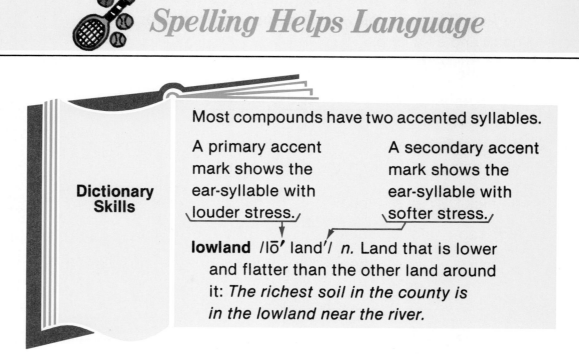

Dictionary Skills

Most compounds have two accented syllables.

A **primary accent** mark shows the ear-syllable with louder stress.

A **secondary accent** mark shows the ear-syllable with softer stress.

lowland /lō′ land′/ *n.* Land that is lower and flatter than the other land around it: *The richest soil in the county is in the lowland near the river.*

1. Write a dictionary entry for **stronghold,** including the pronunciation, part of speech, definition, and sentence. Compare the entry you write with the entry in the Spelling Dictionary.

_____

_____

_____

 2. **Proofread** the sentences below. Write them correctly. Underline each compound with a primary accent on the second syllable.

   a. jane ate all six pancake herself

   b. we turned handsprings beside the drivway

_____

_____

Dingle Jingle

If **genuine breakfast food** is "real oatmeal," what's a **western carriage insect?**

_____

Sound out the long-vowel and short-vowel compounds.

grapevine	hindsight	oatmeal	fusebox	suitcase
raindrop	limestone	hitchhike	newsreel	bluebell
goldfinch	showboat	highway	skyline	handbag
themselves	thumbtack	landscape	offside	wishbone

The numbered sentences are double-talk. The lettered sentences are their real meanings. Match the sentence letters with the correct sentence numbers.

1. Never change horses in midstream. _____

2. Into each lifetime a few raindrops must fall. _____

3. Do not expect somebody else to pull your chestnuts out of the fire. _____

4. The grapevine says you will win by a landslide. _____

5. We see daylight at the end of the tunnel. _____

A. All people have to suffer some evils.

B. Do not look for others to get you out of trouble.

C. When you have reasons for what you are doing, do not change too quickly.

D. We see hope for the future.

E. It is secretly said that you will win easily.

Test

17

4 Pool Crawl Spellings

soot
nook

booth
troop
groove

sprout
drought
brow
browse
bough Ⓗ

foil
toil
broil

hawk
sprawl
clause
staunch
scald
squall
Ⓢ cough

Some vowel sounds have two-letter spellings.

/u̇/ *oo*   /ü/ *oo*

/ou/ *ou, ow*   /oi/ *oi*

/ȯ/ *au, aw, a(l)*

1. Write the /ȯ/ and /oi/ words. Underline the snurk.

_____

_____

_____

2. Write the /ou/ words. Circle the homonym of **bow.**

_____

_____

3. Write the **oo** words. Underline the /u̇/ words.

_____

4. Write the words with these spellings.

   a. s spells /z/   **b. gh** spells /f/   **c. gh** is silent

_____

Working with the Words

1. Write synonyms from the spelling list for these words.

   a. branch   **b.** firm   **c.** forehead

_____

   d. storm   **e.** group   **f.** rut

_____

   g. work   **h.** burn   **i.** dryness

_____

2. Write the correct word for each sentence.

   a. A quiet corner of a room is a ___ . (/grüv/, /nu̇k/)

   b. A tree limb is a ___ . (/bou/, /brou/)

_____

3. Write the plural form of each pictured noun.

a.   **b.**   **c.**

_____

soot
nook
booth
troop
groove
sprout
drought
brow
browse
bough
foil
toil
broil
hawk
sprawl
clause
staunch
scald
squall
cough

4. Proofread the sentences. Write the sentences using spelling words to fill the spaces. Capitalize and punctuate the sentences correctly.

a. robin hood had fine schemes to ___ his foes

_____

_____

b. we have been ___ friends for a long time

_____

_____

c. a few seeds did not ___ during the ___

_____

_____

d. wrapping gumdrops in ___ will keep them fresh

_____

_____

e. do boys like to ___ in old toy shops

_____

_____

f. ___ have strong wings and long claws

_____

_____

5. Write verbs from the list for these pictures.

a.   b.   c.

Look at the picture on page 18. What are the five basic strokes in swimming? Write a short story about how you learned to swim.

Spelling Helps Language

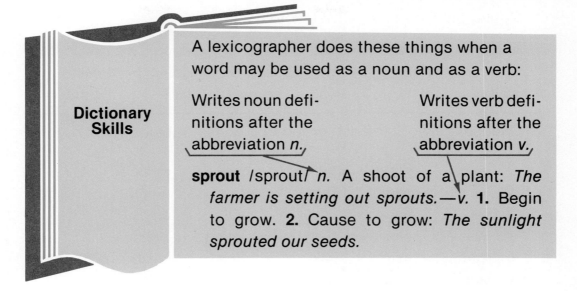

Dictionary Skills

A lexicographer does these things when a word may be used as a noun and as a verb:

Writes noun definitions after the abbreviation *n.*

Writes verb definitions after the abbreviation *v.*

sprout /sprout/ *n.* A shoot of a plant: *The farmer is setting out sprouts.* —*v.* **1.** Begin to grow. **2.** Cause to grow: *The sunlight sprouted our seeds.*

1. Write a dictionary entry for the word **troop.** Write noun and verb definitions and two sample sentences.

_____

_____

_____

2. The **subject** tells what a sentence is about. The **predicate** tells about the subject. Match subjects from Box A with predicates from Box B to write three sentences. Underline the /ô/ and /ou/ words.

A. The small house

Soot

Ben and Paul

B. sprawled on the couch.

is on the brow of the hill.

makes smoke black.

_____

_____

_____

_____

Sound out these two-vowel words.

loop	hood	ounce	prow	stoop	wool
roost	trout	scowl	soil	drawl	naught
waltz	point	yawn	cause	bald	launch

Choose the word in each group that does not belong.

1. hood — shawl — (blouse) — cape — cloak
2. hand — neck — fist — wrist — thumb
3. pool — pond — lake — gulf — brook
4. inch — ounce — foot — pound — length
5. stump — elm — oak — pine — beech
6. launch — cruise — boat — ship — skiff
7. flock — troop — crew — team — class
8. bake — cook — broil — singe — roast
9. brown — green — white — black — blue
10. tea — oil — milk — juice — broth
11. trout — bass — goldfish — catfish — sunfish
12. hawk — crane — gull — duck — goose
13. moth — ant — louse — frog — roach
14. fawn — moose — stag — hound — elk
15. vault — jog — trot — race — sprint

Dingle Jingle

If a **bird complaint** is a "hawk squawk," what's a **bird frown?**

_____

Test

5 Pole-Vault Compounds

We spell the word parts in compounds as we spell one-syllable words.

*Find every two-letter vowel spelling option in the **Pole-Vault** spelling list.*

mushroom
toothbrush
foolproof
fishhook
footstep
footstool
blowout
outline
soundproof
browbeat
however
oilcan
tinfoil
dauntless
saucepan
drawback
lawnmower
falsehood
downfall
doughnut

1. Write the six compounds with /ou/. Underline each word part in which **ow** spells /ou/.

_____

_____

2. Write the six compounds with /ô/. Underline each word part in which **a** before **l** spells /ô/.

_____

_____

3. Write the compounds with /oi/. Underline each word part in which **oi** spells /oi/.

_____

4. Write the compounds with **oo.** Underline the word parts in which **oo** spells /u̇/.

_____

_____

5. Write the picture words. Circle the snurk.

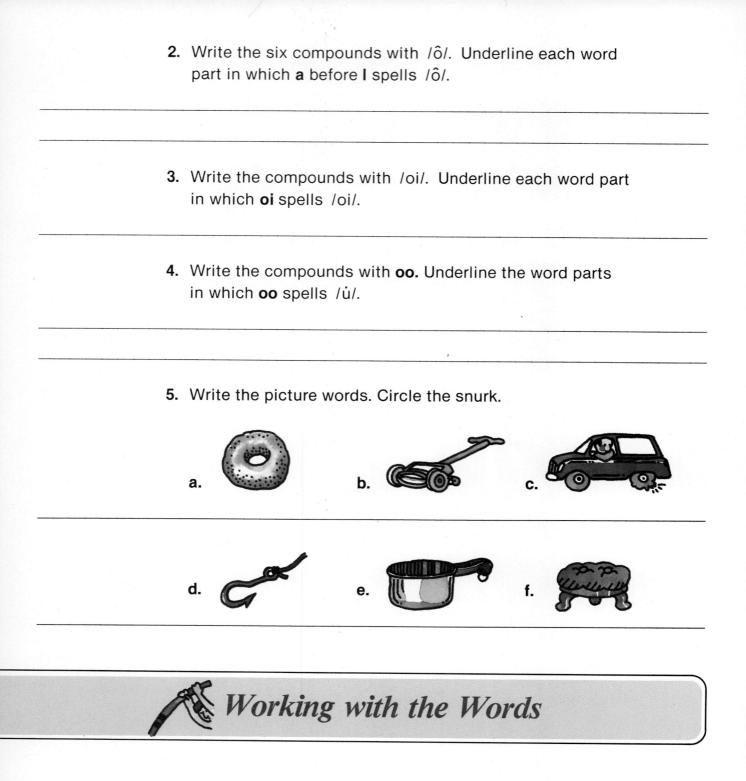

a.   b.   c.

_____

d.   e.   f.

_____

Working with the Words

1. Write a sentence using the compound noun **drawback.** Then write another sentence using the two words **draw** and **back.** Proofread your sentences.

_____

_____

2. Write a sentence using the noun **downfall** and another sentence using the words **fall** and **down.**

_____

_____

_____

The word **however** is used as a conjunction to connect two sentences. We use a semicolon (;) between the connected sentences and a comma (,) after **however.**

We were late; however, no one scolded us.

3. Write connected sentences using **however.** Write about someone who thinks that baiting a fishhook is a drawback to the fun of fishing.

_____

_____

4. Join words in Box A with picture words in Box B to form six compound words.

A. foot	oil
sauce	false
dough	tooth

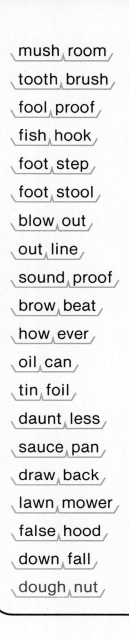

B.		

_____

_____

Dingle Jingle

If **silent shingles** are a "soundproof roof," what's a **notebook robber?**

_____

25

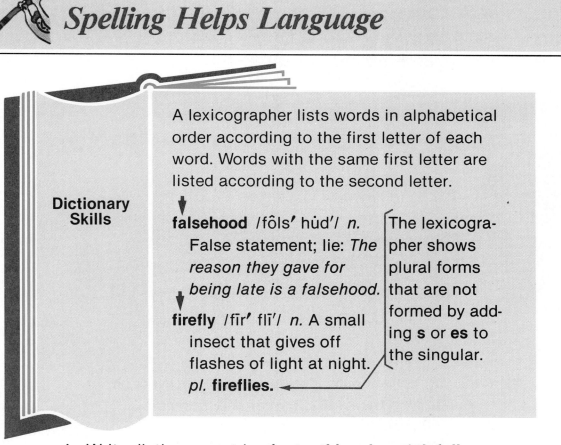

Dictionary Skills

A lexicographer lists words in alphabetical order according to the first letter of each word. Words with the same first letter are listed according to the second letter.

falsehood /fôls′ hůd′/ *n.* False statement; lie: *The reason they gave for being late is a falsehood.*

firefly /fīr′ flī′/ *n.* A small insect that gives off flashes of light at night. *pl.* **fireflies.**

The lexicographer shows plural forms that are not formed by adding **s** or **es** to the singular.

1. Write dictionary entries for **toothbrush** and **tinfoil.** Put the entries in alphabetical order.

_____

_____

_____

_____

_____

2. Unscramble the word parts and write six compounds.

sawshop	whiskout	driftcloth
pawnbroom	oilwood	dugdust

_____

_____

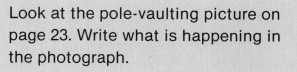

Look at the pole-vaulting picture on page 23. Write what is happening in the photograph.

Sound out the compounds with two-letter vowel spellings.

joyride	downstream	drawstring	boyhood
crawfish	pinpoint	uproot	plywood
causeway	ballroom	cowboy	roundup
looseleaf	lawsuit	softball	household

Proofread these sentences. Find mistakes in spelling (S), punctuation (P), capital letters (C), use of English (E), and fact (F). For each sentence write the total number of each kind of mistake. Then write the sentences correctly. The mistakes have been counted for the first sentence.

1. Pancakes, mushrooms Oatmeal, and toadstools is good breakfast foods.

   S _____ P __1__ C __1__ E __1__ F __2__

2. Cowhands brand livestock at roundups in the southwest

   S _____ P _____ C _____ E _____ F _____

3. Softball is offen played on playgrounds bye our classmates.

   S _____ P _____ C _____ E _____ F _____

4. Daniel boone, in his coonskin cap, become an outlaw in the backwoods of Texas.

   S _____ P _____ C _____ E _____ F _____

5. Newsboys may not sell papers downtown.

   S _____ P _____ C _____ E _____ F _____

6. Scoutmaster's can allways be proud of scouts who tell falsehoods.

   S _____ P _____ C _____ E _____ F _____

7. Loseleaf notebooks can be found in many classrooms.

   S _____ P _____ C _____ E _____ F _____

Test

6 Hurl the Spear Words

spark
snarl
starve

blare
stairs

term
merge
squirt
whir
curb
spur

thorn
ore
hoard
coarse Ⓗ

smear
shears
sneer
jeer
Ⓢ *fierce*

Vowel-r sounds have these spelling options:

/är/ *ar*	/ãr/ *are, air*
/ėr/ *er, ir, ur*	/ôr/ *or, ore, oar*
/ir/ *ear, eer*	

1. Write the /ėr/ words. Underline the vowel-r letters.

28

2. Write the /ir/ words, including the snurk. Underline the vowel-**r** letters.

_____

_____

3. Write the /är/ and /ãr/ words. Circle the /ãr/ words.

_____

_____

4. Write the words with these pronunciations.

   a. /hôrd/   **b.** /ôr/   **c.** /thôrn/

_____

5. Write **coarse** and its homonym **course.** Underline the word that means "not fine or smooth."

_____

6. Write the **ing** forms of **merge, blare,** and **starve.** Drop the final silent **e** before adding the ending.

_____

Working with the Words

1. Write the two plural nouns that are in the list and the plural form of **ore.**

_____

2. Write the picture words and their correct sound spellings.

   a.   **b.**   **c.**

   /ŦHôrnz/ or /thôrnz/   /kėrb/ or /kůrb/   /snãrl/ or /snärl/

_____

3. An **antonym** is a word that means the opposite, or nearly the opposite, of another word. Write antonyms from the spelling list for these words.

    a. mild   **b.** smooth   **c.** part

    d. waste   **e.** feast   **f.** purr

4. Write words from the list for these meanings.

    a. hold back   **b.** make fun of   **c.** blur

Spelling Helps Language

The adjective endings **er** and **est** mean "more" and "most."

Fiercer means "more fierce."

Fiercest means "most fierce."

1. Write words meaning "more hoarse" and "most coarse."

2. The picture words have the same vowel-**r** spellings as the printed partner words. Write the picture words.

      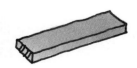

    a. spark   **b.** ore   **c.** hoard

spark
snarl
starve
blare
stairs
term
merge
squirt
whir
curb
spur
thorn
ore
hoard
coarse
smear
shears
sneer
jeer
fierce

Dictionary Skills

A lexicographer may write only a **phrase,** or sentence part, to show how an entry word is used.

A lexicographer shows the **er** and **est** forms of adjectives that drop final **e** before the endings.

coarse /kôrs/ *adj.* **1.** Not fine: *coarse hair.* **2.** Rough: *coarse cloth.* **3.** Poor: *coarse food.* **4.** Crude: *coarse manners.*   **coarser, coarsest.**

3. Write a dictionary entry for **scarce.** Write a sample phrase. Show **er** and **est** endings.

_____

_____

_____

4. Write two connected sentences about Marge who ripped her sleeve on a thorny bush, but did not hurt her arm. Use **however** and several vowel-**r** words. Use the semicolon correctly.

_____

_____

Look again at the picture on page 28. In a few sentences describe how a javelin is thrown at track and field meets.

Dingle Jingle

If a **rectangular rabbit** is a "square hare," what are **unusual twins?**

_____

31

Sound out these vowel-**r** words. Then read the story.

dwarf	score	burst	sear	board	hurl
shark	hoarse	gear	glare	clerk	spear
flair	verse	steer	forge	whirl	cheer

Of course you recall the fable of the fox and the grapes. The fox tried hard to jump up and grab the ripe grapes. When the thwarted fox failed, he glared at them and snarled, "Who cares? The grapes are sour!"

Two large birds — a pair of crows — were perched in a tall fir tree nearby, peering at the scene below.

"Hear that, my dear?" jeered the first crow scornfully. "What a bad sport!"

"Cheer up, Claire," sneered her spouse. "We're far smarter than the foxes, and we never try to kid ourselves. Let's get started and get our share of that farmer's corn!"

Just as they darted after the ears of corn, the farmer's rear door slammed. He burst forth from his back porch. His shotgun roared. The scared crows soared off in a hurry.

"Oh, well," snorted Claire, "the corn is too green to eat. We've just spared ourselves a bad case of heartburn."

Now what is the moral of this fable?

How many vowel-**r** words are in the story? _____

Test

7 Surfboard Compounds

We spell the word parts in compounds as we spell one-syllable words. Find every vowel-r spelling option in the **Surfboard Compounds** spelling list.

farmhouse
trademark
yardstick

carefree
spareribs
airline
stairway

iceberg
outskirts
turnstile
surfboard

forbid
shortstop
forecast
bookstore
billboard

peerless
spearmint
earring

S therefore

1. Write the snurk and the compounds with /ãr/ or /är/. Circle the snurk.

_____

_____

farm house
trade mark
yard stick
care free
spare ribs
air line
stair way
ice berg
out skirts
turn stile
surf board
for bid
short stop
fore cast
book store
bill board
peer less
spear mint
ear ring
there fore

2. Write the compounds with /ėr/ or /ir/. Underline the word that means "without equal."

_____

_____

3. Write the compounds with /ôr/. Circle the adverb.

_____

_____

4. Write the words with these spellings and sounds.

    a. ss = /s/   **b. th** = /ŦH/   **c. ck** = /k/

_____

    d. ll = /l/   **e. c** = /s/   **f. s** = /z/

_____

Working with the Words

1. Write **forecast, forbid,** and **therefore.** Underline the syllables with a primary accent.

_____

2. Write the spelling words for these pictures. Underline the syllables with a primary accent.

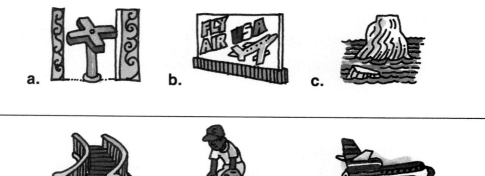

a.   b.   c.

_____

d.   e.   f.

_____

3. Unscramble the word parts to write eight compounds from the spelling list.

sparehouse spearribs outmark airmint

earskirts   foreline   farmring tradecast

_____

_____

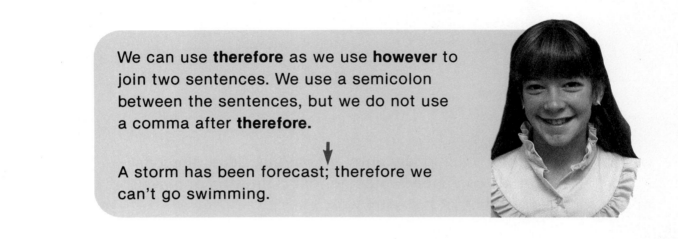

We can use **therefore** as we use **however** to join two sentences. We use a semicolon between the sentences, but we do not use a comma after **therefore.**

A storm has been forecast; therefore we can't go swimming.

4. Use compound words from the spelling list in these sentences. Write the sentences with correct capitalization and punctuation.

 a. our team has no ____ therefore we can't play baseball.

_____

_____

 b. which ____ has a large landing field on the ____ of our City.

_____

_____

 c. small ____ Plants are sprouting near the ____.

_____

_____

 d. ____ make a ____ meal.

_____

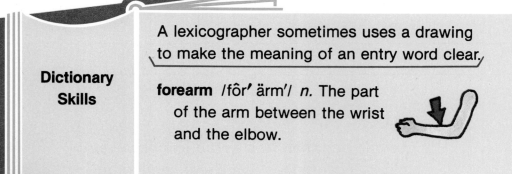

Dictionary Skills

A lexicographer sometimes uses a drawing to make the meaning of an entry word clear.

forearm /fôr′ ärm′/ *n.* The part of the arm between the wrist and the elbow.

1. Write a dictionary entry for **earring.** Do all the jobs a lexicographer would do. Use a drawing to make the meaning of the entry word clear.

2. Join words from Box A with words from Box B to form six new compounds.

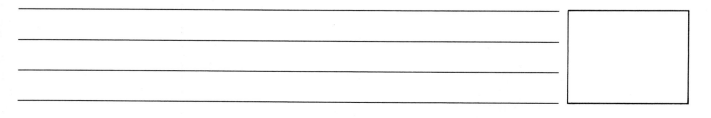

A. for　fore　fear

tear　out　store

B. less　drop　tell

get　smart　room

Look again at the picture on page 33. Write why all surfboard riders should be good swimmers.

Sound out the vowel-**r** compounds.

forearm	wardrobe	deerskin	shorthand	horseback
longhorn	earphone	gearshift	outsmart	birdhouse
herself	fairgrounds	warfare	yearbook	cardboard

Choose the word in each row that does not belong. Tell why.

1. strawstack	longhorn	roundup	cowboy
2. billboard	scoreboard	shortstop	grandstand
3. turnpike	sidewalk	trademark	driveway
4. textbook	chalkboard	barefoot	schoolyard
5. raindrop	iceberg	hailstone	snowflake
6. sharpshooter	quarterback	cheerleader	cornerback
7. stagecoach	airplane	streetcar	cartwheel
8. popcorn	fruitcake	charcoal	doughnut
9. storeroom	warehouse	wardrobe	yardstick
10. farewell	forenoon	midnight	noonday
11. sparkplug	carport	gearshift	dashboard
12. foreman	chairman	shareholder	ringleader
13. whirlwind	snowstorm	cloudburst	lukewarm
14. eardrum	forehead	forearm	haircut
15. hardware	scarecrow	pitchfork	barnyard

Dingle Jingle

If a **country pest** is a "farmhouse mouse,"
what's a **happy honey-maker**?

_____

Test

8 *Major Hockey Rivals*

buckle
tremble
rival
oval
panel
vessel
civil
nostril
pistol

blister
grocer
molar
cedar
vapor
major

weary
husky
hockey
barley
 honey

Spelling options for soft-syllable endings:

/əl/ *le, al, el, il, ol*

/ər/ *er, ar, or*

/ē/ *y, ey*

1. Write the /ē/-ending words. Circle the snurk and the word that names a grain.

2. Write the /əl/ words in alphabetical order.

_____

_____

3. Write the /ər/ words in alphabetical order.

_____

4. Write the picture words. Underline the singular word.

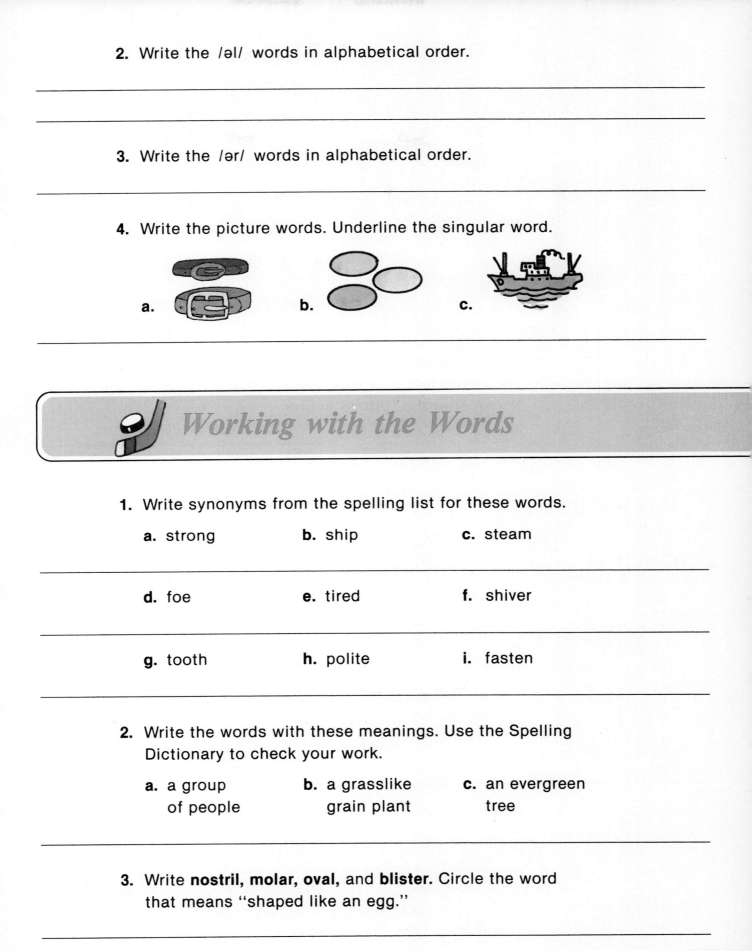

a.　　　　　b.　　　　　c.

Working with the Words

1. Write synonyms from the spelling list for these words.

　a. strong　　　**b.** ship　　　**c.** steam

_____

　d. foe　　　**e.** tired　　　**f.** shiver

_____

　g. tooth　　　**h.** polite　　　**i.** fasten

_____

2. Write the words with these meanings. Use the Spelling Dictionary to check your work.

　a. a group of people　　**b.** a grasslike grain plant　　**c.** an evergreen tree

_____

3. Write **nostril, molar, oval,** and **blister.** Circle the word that means "shaped like an egg."

_____

39

buck le
trem ble
ri val
o val
pan el
ves sel
civ il
nos tril
pis tol
blis ter
gro cer
mo lar
ce dar
va por
ma jor
wear y
hus ky
hock ey
bar ley
hon ey

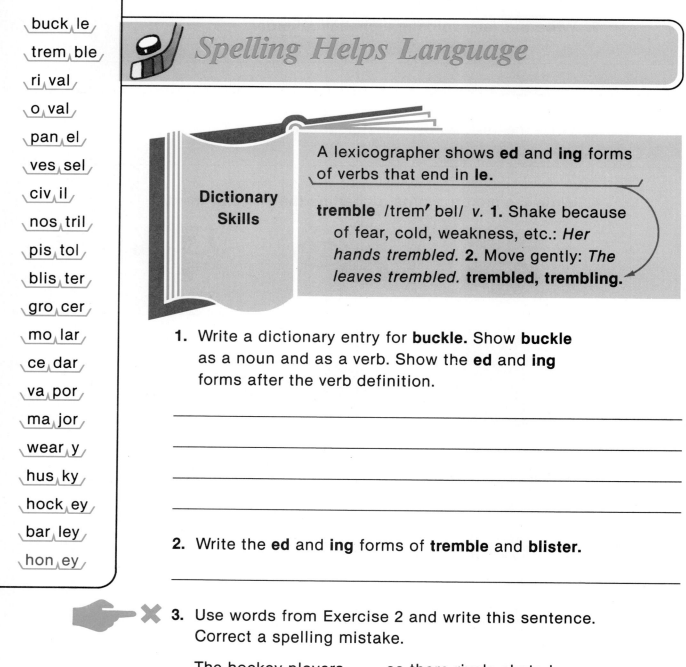

Spelling Helps Language

Dictionary Skills

A lexicographer shows **ed** and **ing** forms of verbs that end in **le**.

tremble /trem′ bəl/ *v.* **1.** Shake because of fear, cold, weakness, etc.: *Her hands trembled.* **2.** Move gently: *The leaves trembled.* **trembled, trembling.**

1. Write a dictionary entry for **buckle**. Show **buckle** as a noun and as a verb. Show the **ed** and **ing** forms after the verb definition.

_____

_____

_____

_____

2. Write the **ed** and **ing** forms of **tremble** and **blister**.

_____

 3. Use words from Exercise 2 and write this sentence. Correct a spelling mistake.

The hockey players ___ as there rivals skated toward them with ___ speed.

_____

_____

_____

Write a short story about the hockey picture on page 38. You are the player who is about to slam the puck. What happened? Who won?

Sound out the words. Then read the story.

donkey	pickle	final	jockey	humble	fatal
nickel	traitor	yodel	scissors	easel	splendor
collar	peril	polar	stencil	freezer	kennel

Did you ever read the fable of the crafty fox and the vain crow? The sneaky rascal flattered the silly crow who held a morsel of creamy cheese in her beak. The wily scoundrel wheedled the crow into favoring him with a song because, he said, she had such a lovely voice. The simpering crow burst into a raspy croak—and dropped her cheese.

"Sucker!" snickered the fox, gobbling up the cheese.

"Mighty clever!" cried the squeaky voice of a tiny mouse from the safety of a bramble bush. Her whiskers quivered and her beady little eyes twinkled eagerly as she sniffed the odor of the cheese. "Fox, level with me. You dazzle one with your brains! What an actor! How did you get so clever?"

The chesty fox closed his eyes, as all deep thinkers do. "It's simple," he said. "I'm smarter because..."

In a flash the nimble mouse had pilfered the cheese!

"Sucker!" she whispered with a chuckle.

Now what is the moral of this fable?

Dingle Jingle

If **polite baloney** is "civil drivel," what's an **arctic tooth?**

_____

Test

plastic
napkin
custom
public
suffix
pardon
dentist
welfare
canvas
gadget
tablet

rocket
nephew

vibrate
sacred

mattress
surplus
△ approve

athlete
sculpture

Eye-syllables are word parts we see. We divide VCCV and VCCCV words into eye-syllables to make them easier to spell.

VC|CV   VCC|V   V|CCV

VC|CCV   VCC|CV

1. Write the VCC|V and V|CCV words. Underline the two words that are used as nouns.

2. Write the ⌄VC⌄CV⌄ words. Underline the word that means "not private."

_____

_____

_____

3. Write the VCCCV words. Underline the words that are divided after the second consonant.

_____

_____

4. Write **athlete, approve, welfare,** and **sculpture.** Underline the accented syllable in each word.

_____

Working with the Words

Both vowel sounds are easy to hear in words like **welfare** and **plastic.**

The vowel sounds are hard to hear in the unaccented syllables of words like **canvas** and **surplus.**

The schwa /ə/ shows the hard-to-hear vowel sound.

/kan′ vəs/   /sėr′ pləs/

1. Write **napkin, vibrate, custom,** and **athlete.** Underline the three words with clear vowel sounds in both syllables.

_____

2. Write the words with these sounds and spellings.

    a. ph = /f/   **b. x** = /ks/   **c. g** = /j/

_____

plas tic

nap kin

cus tom

pub lic

suf fix

par don

den tist

wel fare

can vas

gad get

tab let

rock et

neph ew

vi brate

sa cred

mat tress

sur plus

ap prove

ath lete

sculp ture

Spelling Helps Language

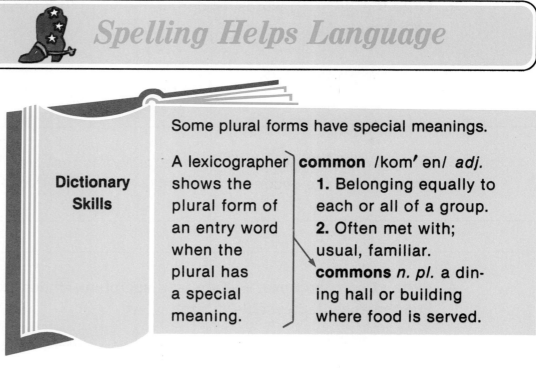

Dictionary Skills

A lexicographer shows the plural form of an entry word when the plural has a special meaning.

Some plural forms have special meanings.

common /kom′ ən/ *adj.*
1. Belonging equally to each or all of a group.
2. Often met with; usual, familiar.
commons *n. pl.* a dining hall or building where food is served.

1. Write a dictionary entry for **custom.** Show one or more special meanings of **customs.** Use your Spelling Dictionary for the facts.

_____

_____

_____

_____

2. Write the plurals of **mattress, canvas, suffix,** and **surplus.** Use the Spelling Dictionary.

_____

3. Write this sentence and mark it *true* or *false.*

A suffix is added to the end of a word.

_____

That's your older brother in the rodeo picture on page 42. In a few words explain what he is doing. (See **Rodeo** in your encyclopedia.)

44

Spelling Helps Reading

Sound out the VCCV and VCCCV words.

eastern	piston	monster	western	sandwich
nugget	banjo	common	distrust	foundry
advance	trumpet	employ	degree	empress
rascal	victim	microbe	eclipse	antlers

Guess the meanings of the boldface words by the way they are used in the sentences. Choose the correct meanings.

1. "We must **maintain** our defenses," said the captain, "or the foe will capture our fortress."

   increase   decrease   keep up

2. "We must maintain our defenses against the foe's **assault**," said the captain, "or they will capture our fortress."

   retreat   attack   plans

3. "We must maintain our defenses against **hostile** assaults," said the captain, "or the foe will capture our fortress."

   friendly   unfriendly   unplanned

4. "We must maintain defenses against **massive** hostile assaults," he said, "or they will capture our fortress."

   heavy   daily   clever

Dingle Jingle

If a **jailer's excuse** is a "warden's pardon," what's a **small missile**?

_____

Test

10 Human Comet Words

slogan
omit
soda
virus
acorn
agent
donate
stupid
tuna
unite
§ plateau

clinic
comet
melon
value
tenant
topic
panic
chorus
§ shovel

We divide **VCV** words into eye-syllables to make them easier to spell.

VC V   lem on   V CV   so da

1. Write the four words that end with a vowel sound. Underline the three letters that spell one sound.

46

2. Write the ⌣V⌃CV⌣ words. Underline the word in which **eau** snurkily spells /ō/.

_____

_____

_____

3. Write the ⌣VC⌃V⌣ words. Underline the word in which **o** snurkily spells /u/.

_____

_____

4. Write the plural of **virus, chorus,** and **plateau.**

_____

5. Write the two words that end with /ə/.

_____

Working with the Words

1. Write the ⌣V⌃CV⌣ words with two long-vowel sounds.

_____

2. Write the ⌣VC⌃V⌣ words with /a/, /e/, or /u/ in the first syllable. Underline the name of a food.

_____

3. Write the words for these pronunciations.

    a. /kôr′ əs/   **b.** /kom′ ət/   **c.** /klin′ ik/

_____

4. Write the two words that end with a long-vowel sound.

_____

47

slo gan
o mit
so da
vi rus
a corn
a gent
do nate
stu pid
tu na
u nite
pla teau
clin ic
com et
mel on
val ue
ten ant
top ic
pan ic
chor us
shov el

Spelling Helps Language

Dictionary Skills

We double the final consonant before adding **ed** and **ing** when a two-syllable word has the accent on the second syllable and ends in one consonant following a single vowel:

admit, admitted, admitting

admit /ad mit′/ v. **1.** Say something is true: *admit a mistake.* **2.** Allow to enter: *Do not admit strangers.* **admitted, admitting.**

A lexicographer shows the **ed** and **ing** forms of verbs when the final consonant is doubled.

1. Write an entry for **omit**. Show the **ed** and **ing** forms. Compare your work with the Spelling Dictionary.

_____

_____

_____

2. Write the **ing** forms of **panic, donate,** and **value.** Use the Spelling Dictionary.

_____

3. Write a sentence about children who join forces to rake leaves at a health clinic. Use the words **united, donated,** and **clinic.**

_____

_____

Imagine you are the TV announcer watching the play in the football picture on page 46. Write what you would tell your audience.

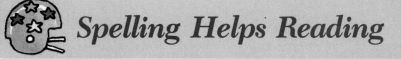

polite	vacant	basin	robot	comic	modest
human	climate	event	talent	credit	punish
basic	silo	humid	civic	widow	menu

Oh, hear now the tale of Elena Corona.
Her Pa was from Frisco. Her Ma? Barcelona!
She had a debate with Terence T. Fagan,
Whose Pa was from Dublin. His Ma? Copenhagen!
Our syllable-slicer (we'll here call her Helen)
Said, "The word isn't ME-lon. Of course it is MEL-on.
We do not say PE-tal. We always say PET-al.
We never say ME-tal. We like to say MET-al.
You do not say RI-vet. You have to say RIV-et.
You must not say PI-vot. You always say PIV-ot.
I insist on my point in this classroom DE-bate.
This is the right way to SYL-lab-i-cate!"
Said Terence, "That's silly. We've got to be PRU-dent.
We never say STUD-ent. We always say STU-dent.
We do not say CUP-id. We've got to say CU-pid.
We dare not say STUP-id. So let's not be STU-pid."
Said Helen, "I'm SPAN-ish. Don't say I am SPA-nish."
Said Terence, "My Mama's not DAN-ish. She's DA-nish."

Dingle Jingle

If a **dull archer** is a "stupid cupid,"
what's a **southern subject**?

_____

Test

11 Slippery Syllables

reptile
puppet
dessert

hatred
fragrance

method
cricket
⧩ leather

perspire
tantrum

cartridge
muskrat

locate
humid
humane

decade
linen
magic

riot
fluid

These are the eight letter patterns that help us break words into eye-syllables.

rep|tile	ha|tred
VC↑CV	V↑CCV
meth|od	per|spire
VCC↑V	VC↑CCV
cart|ridge	lo|cate
VCC↑CV	V↑CV
dec|ade	ri|ot
VC↑V	V↑V

1. Write the VCCV words. Underline the ⌣VCC⌣V⌣ words.

_____

_____

2. Write the VCV words. Underline the ⌣V⌣CV⌣ words.

_____

_____

3. Write the VCCCV words. Underline the ⌣VCC⌣CV⌣ words.

_____

4. Write the words that we divide between two vowels.

_____

5. Write the words with these sounds and spellings.

    a. g spells /j/   **b. c** spells /s/   **c. th** spells /th/

_____

    d. dge spells /j/   **e. ck** spells /k/   **f. th** spells /ŦH/

_____

Working with the Words

1. Write the singular and plural forms of these words.

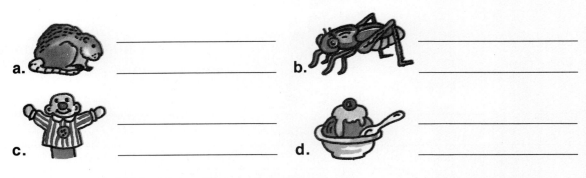

  a. _____   **b.** _____

  c. _____   **d.** _____

2. Write this question and a one-word answer.

   Is **puppet** a word that means "little dog"?

_____

rep tile

pup pet

des sert

ha tred

fra grance

meth od

crick et

leath er

per spire

tan trum

cart ridge

musk rat

lo cate

hu mid

hu mane

dec ade

lin en

mag ic

ri ot

flu id

3. Write the words with these meanings.

a. great dislike　**b.** ten years　**c.** moist; damp

_____

d. fit of　　　**e.** sweet scent　**f.** cloth made
temper　　　　　　　　　　　　　of flax

_____

4. Unscramble the underlined words and write the sentences correctly. Pay close attention to the punctuation marks in the sentences.

a.

"Yes, I will show you <u>making method for my puppets with linen</u> and leather," said Dot.

_____

_____

b.

"Yes, I think certain <u>found may in reptiles be</u> the desert," declared Henry.

_____

_____

c.

"What <u>day humid a</u>!" groaned the perspiring man.

_____

_____

Look again at the picture on page 50. Explain in your own words what the man on the log is doing.

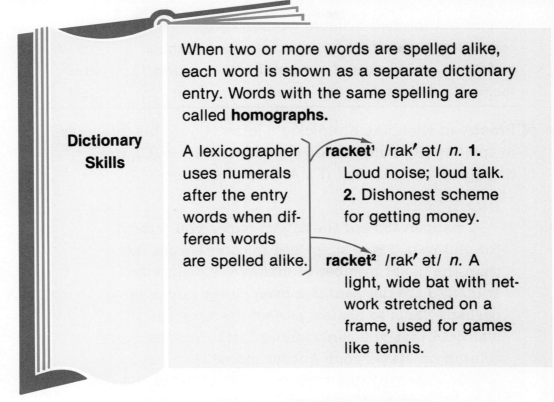

When two or more words are spelled alike, each word is shown as a separate dictionary entry. Words with the same spelling are called **homographs.**

Dictionary Skills

A lexicographer uses numerals after the entry words when different words are spelled alike.

racket¹ /rak′ ət/ *n.* **1.** Loud noise; loud talk. **2.** Dishonest scheme for getting money.

racket² /rak′ ət/ *n.* A light, wide bat with network stretched on a frame, used for games like tennis.

1. Write two dictionary entries for **cricket** and number them. Find the information in the Spelling Dictionary, but use your own words to write the entries.

_____

_____

_____

_____

2. Write a declarative sentence using **cricket** (the insect) and a question using **cricket** (the English game).

_____

_____

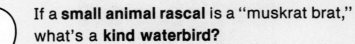

Dingle Jingle

If a **small animal rascal** is a "muskrat brat," what's a **kind waterbird?**

_____

Sound out the two-syllable words.

collide	patrol	bucket	fortress	vanish
mistake	fragment	nostril	actress	ideal
success	locket	hamster	unit	duel

Proofread Nicholas Knitpicker's letter. Count his mistakes in spelling (S), punctuation (P), capitalization (C), use of English (E), and fact (F). Answer his letter.

Dear Editer:

I happen to read the school paper you publish for children. I was surprised to come across more than the usual number of mistake. I realize that student's are not geniuses even clever pupils is perhaps liable to neglect perfect grammer. I maintain that you can't ignore facts. In your quiz column on states your Author stated that:

1. The state with the most counties is Texas. Its got to be New York.
2. Theres only one State with a one-syllable name. I managed to locate too.
3. There is eight states that begin with the letter M. I find only seven.
4. The quiz asked: "Is it legal in New York for a husband to marry his widows sister. This is stupid. Of coarse he can.

Nicholas Knitpicker

How many mistakes?

S _____ P _____ C _____ E _____ F _____

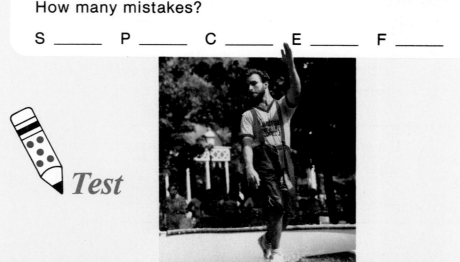

Test

54

12 Track Practice Words

Hear /a/ in **fact** and in the accented syllable of each two-syllable word in the **Track Practice** list.

We spell /a/ with the vowel letter a.

fact
swamp

crafty
galley

chapter
actor
grammar
hangar ⒣

tackle
camel
scandal

knapsack
backtrack

atlas
cactus
practice

hatchet
anthem

atom
static

1. Write the words pronounced /fakt/, /swomp/, and /hang′ ər/. Circle the snurk.

fact
swamp
craf‚ty
gal‚ley
chap‚ter
ac‚tor
gram‚mar
hang‚ar
tack‚le
cam‚el
scan‚dal
knap‚sack
back‚track
at‚las
cac‚tus
prac‚tice
hat‚chet
an‚them
at‚om
stat‚ic

2. Write the words with the /ər/, /əl/, or /ē/ endings.

_____

_____

3. Write the compound words. Underline the verb.

_____

4. Write the ‿VC‚CV‿ words with these pronunciations.

   a. /at′ ləs/   **b.** /kak′ təs/   **c.** /prak′ təs/

_____

5. Write the ‿VC‚CCV‿ words with these pronunciations.

   a. /hat′ chət/   **b.** /an′ thəm/

_____

6. Write the ‿VC‚V‿ words with these pronunciations.

   a. /at′ əm/   **b.** /stat′ ik/

_____

Working with the Words

1. Write a word from the spelling list for each box.

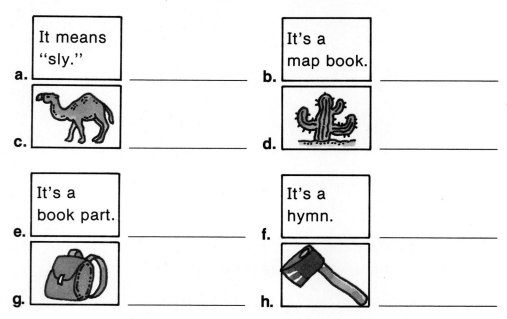

  a. It means "sly." _____

  b. It's a map book. _____

  c. _____

  d. _____

  e. It's a book part. _____

  f. It's a hymn. _____

  g. _____

  h. _____

Spelling Helps Language

Dictionary Skills

A lexicographer sometimes gives information in a short paragraph after the definition.

camel /kam′ əl/ *n.* A large four-footed mammal with cushioned feet and a long neck. It is used as a beast of burden in the deserts of northern Africa and central Asia.

1. Write a dictionary entry for **atlas,** giving information in a sentence or two following the definition. Use the Spelling Dictionary for facts, but write the entry in your own words.

_____

_____

_____

_____

2. Unscramble the underlined words and write the sentences correctly. Correct two punctuation mistakes.

"No I can't <u>play</u> <u>the</u> <u>for</u> <u>practice</u>! <u>swamped</u> <u>with</u> <u>I'm</u> <u>schoolwork</u>, cried Hank.

_____

_____

Mark a take-off line on the playground. Do three long jumps. Write a short report about the best of your three jumps. Which boy and which girl made the longest jump?

Spelling Helps Reading

Sound out the /a/ words. Then read the story.

rank	panel	graph	anchor	axle	grandstand
lanky	adapt	shabby	cancel	sandal	savage
tractor	rascal	alley	valley	canvas	gangplank

"I think perhaps I'll get this fancy atlas for my dad's birthday, Fran," said Jack Gantry to his friend Fran Hampton. "He travels a lot. I've managed to save up the cash to get it."

"It's a dandy," admitted Fran, casually passing her hand over the satiny plastic jacket on the handsome book.

Jack paid Mrs. Landon and packed the massive book in his canvas knapsack. On the way home Jack yanked the atlas out to glance at the colored maps. Then it happened! The book slipped from his frantic grasp. As he grabbed at it, he tore six pages right out of the brand-new book.

"Let's go back fast," snapped Jack.

Back in the bookshop, he gave the book to Mrs. Landon.

"This atlas is badly damaged, ma'am," he gasped. "See that? I demand a new one. It was torn when I got it. Isn't that a fact, Fran?"

What do you think Fran said? Write your own ending.

Dingle Jingle

If a **Texas mansion** is a "Dallas Palace," what's a **West Texas rope?**

_____

Test

13 Splendid Defense Words

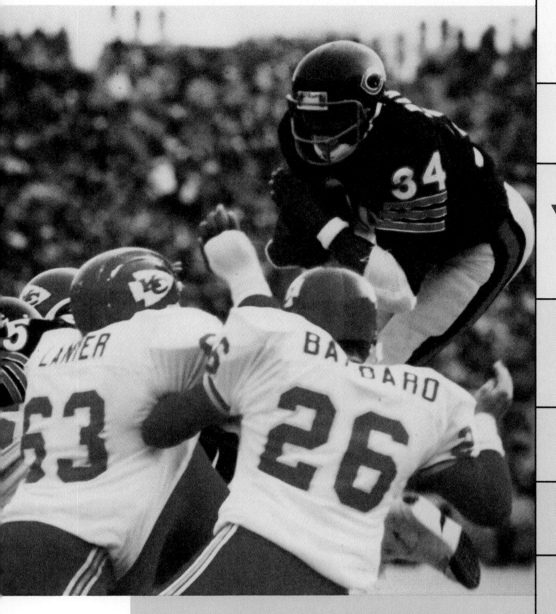

bench
cell Ⓗ

plenty
envy

member
Ⓢ *sweater*
splendor
nectar

freckle
rebel
stencil

themselves
endless

neglect
metric

exit
presence

elect
defense
detect

Hear /e/ in bench, in cell, and in the accented syllable of each two-syllable word in the Splendid Defense list.

We spell /e/ with the vowel letter e.

1. Write the words pronounced /sel/ and /bench/. Underline the word with two consonant sounds.

bench

cell

plen ty

en vy

mem ber

sweat er

splen dor

nec tar

freck le

reb el

sten cil

them selves

end less

neg lect

met ric

ex it

pres ence

e lect

de fense

de tect

2. Write the /əl/-ending and /ē/-ending words.

_____

_____

3. Write the /ər/-ending words, including a snurk.

_____

4. Write the compounds. Underline the word that is a plural pronoun.

_____

5. Write the words with these pronunciations.

   a. /ek′ sit/   **b.** /prez′ əns/   **c.** /ē lekt′/

_____

   d. /dē fens′/   **e.** /dē tekt′/   **f.** /reb′ əl/

_____

6. Write the VC CV words **metric** and **neglect.** Write the **ing** form of /nə glekt′/.

_____

2 Working with the Words

1. Write the snurks **leather, sweater,** and **weather.** Underline the word that rhymes with **better.**

_____

2. Write the picture words.

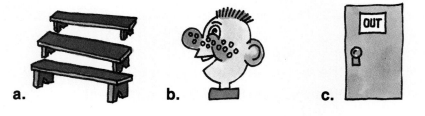

   a.   **b.**   **c.**

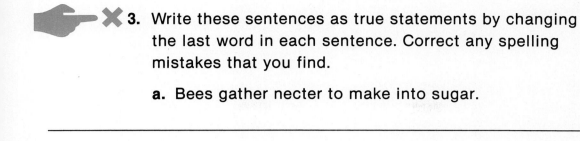 **3.** Write these sentences as true statements by changing the last word in each sentence. Correct any spelling mistakes that you find.

    a. Bees gather necter to make into sugar.

_____

_____

    b. The antonym of **absense** is **presents.**

_____

    c. The way out of a biulding is usually labeled an entrance.

_____

_____

    d. The metric system is a way of measuring that counts by twelve.

_____

_____

    e. A garage for plains is a hanger.

_____

4. Write the unit words with meanings <u>opposite</u> to these.

    a. not enough   **b.** with an ending

    c. take good care of   **d.** defeat by vote

_____

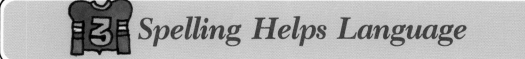 *Spelling Helps Language*

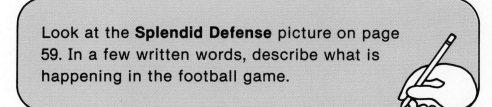 Look at the **Splendid Defense** picture on page 59. In a few written words, describe what is happening in the football game.

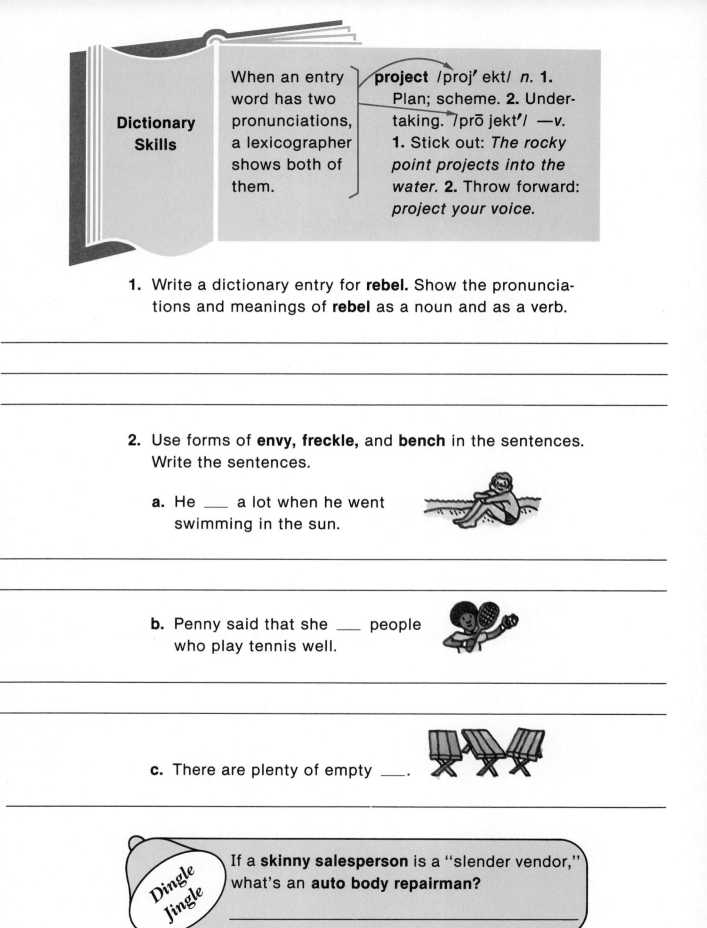

Dictionary Skills

When an entry word has two pronunciations, a lexicographer shows both of them.

project /proj′ ekt/ *n.* **1.** Plan; scheme. **2.** Undertaking. /prō jekt′/ —*v.* **1.** Stick out: *The rocky point projects into the water.* **2.** Throw forward: *project your voice.*

1. Write a dictionary entry for **rebel.** Show the pronunciations and meanings of **rebel** as a noun and as a verb.

_____

_____

_____

2. Use forms of **envy, freckle,** and **bench** in the sentences. Write the sentences.

   a. He ___ a lot when he went swimming in the sun.

_____

_____

   b. Penny said that she ___ people who play tennis well.

_____

_____

   c. There are plenty of empty ___.

_____

Dingle Jingle

If a **skinny salesperson** is a "slender vendor," what's an **auto body repairman?**

_____

Spelling Helps Reading

Sound out the /e/ words. Then read the story.

dwell	messy	vendor	devil	helmet	dentist
drench	tender	cellar	tennis	cement	melon
penny	mental	temple	emblem	erect	lettuce

"Kenneth," yelled Mrs. Clemens, "better answer the phone. I'm expecting a call from Bess Henderson. Take the message for me. We're playing tennis this weekend."

"You get it, Ethel," said Mr. Clemens. "That old pest, Henry Bender, expects me to help him mend the dents in his fenders. If that fellow is on the line, invent an excuse for me. Tell him I'm spending the day at the dentist's."

"Don't ask me to pull your chestnuts out of the fire," said Mrs. Clemens. "You upset me. I do not relish telling lies—even little white ones. I will not rescue you."

"Don't stir up a tempest in a teapot, Ethel. A gentle fib is never a genuine lie."

Mr. Clemens and Helen, his daughter, had settled down to checkers when the phone rang again. Helen answered.

"Hello," said a trembling voice. "Is that you, Helen? This is Mr. Bender. Is your father there?"

What do you think Helen said? Write your own ending.

How many different /e/ words are in the story? _____

Test

14 Gym Whiz Syllables

glimpse
myth
hymn ⓗ
ⓢ sieve

simply
chimney

finger
scissors
pillar

single
shrivel

fingerprint
within

system
missile

liquid
resist

prison
rigid
driven

Hear the /i/ vowel sound in every word in the Gym Whiz list.

We spell /i/ with ℐ and ℳ.

1. Write the one-syllable words. Circle the homonym of the word **him.** Underline the letters that spell /i/ in the snurk.

2. Write the two compounds.

_____

3. Write the two-syllable words with these sounds and spellings.

    a. y = /i/   **b.** y = /ē/   **c.** ey = /ē/

_____

    d. ile = /əl/   **e.** el = /əl/   **f.** le = /əl/

_____

    g. or = /ər/   **h.** ar = /ər/   **i.** er = /ər/

_____

4. Write the words with these pronunciations.

    a. /lik′ wid/   **b.** /rē zist′/   **c.** /priz′ ən/

_____

    d. /rij′ əd/   **e.** /driv′ ən/   **f.** /fing′ gər/

_____

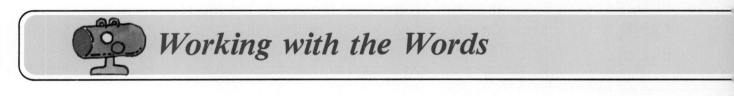

Working with the Words

1. Write the picture words and their plural forms. Use the Spelling Dictionary.

    a.   **b.**   **c.**

_____

_____

2. Write the words with these meanings.

    a. not solid   **b.** only one   **c.** shrink

_____

glimpse
myth
hymn
sieve
sim ply
chim ney
fin ger
scis sors
pil lar
sin gle
shriv el
fin ger print
with in
sys tem
mis sile
li quid
re sist
pris on
rig id
driv en

Spelling Helps Language

Dictionary Skills

We form the past tense of many verbs by adding **ed** or **d** to the root:

| twist — twisted | dine — dined |

We form the past tense of irregular verbs by changing the spelling of the root:

| buy — bought | ride — rode |

A lexicographer shows the past tense of irregular verbs.

send /send/ *v.* **1.** Cause to go. **2.** Drive; throw: *send a ball; send smoke into the air.* **sent, sending.**

1. Write a dictionary entry for the verb **drive.** Show the form for the past tense and the **ing** form. Check your work with the Spelling Dictionary.

_____

_____

_____

2. Write the past tense of each verb.

   a. give   **b.** sit   **c.** bring

   _____

   d. swim   **e.** ring   **f.** begin

   _____

Look again at the picture on page 64. Write a note listing the four gymnastic events in meets for girls.

Sound out the /i/ words. Then read the story.

cinder	lily	shrimp	victor	swivel	twist
vigor	windmill	wintry	dribble	fidget	vivid
gym	victim	dingy	signal	skillet	primer

"Billy Miller, this is the fifth or sixth time you've come without finishing a single problem you were given to do!" said Miss Clifford briskly. "You need some drill."

"I did fiddle around a little," admitted Billy with a timid grin. "I'll never set the river on fire in math."

"Here's a list of problems. Do them on the chalkboard. And you, Cindy Smithers, stay after school, too, and make up your spelling. I'll dismiss you two when you finish."

The two children pitched in. Miss Clifford left the room to get some picnic tickets from the office.

"You're a math whiz," whispered Billy. "Help me."

Within a few minutes Cindy had scribbled the answers and was quickly back at her seat near the window. Miss Clifford came in and squinted at the chalkboard.

"Splendid! Do you think Billy will be able to keep up with the class now, Cindy?" she asked.

What did Cindy say? Write your ending to the story.

Dingle Jingle

If **rhyming words** are a "Dingle Jingle," what's a **one roof tile?**

_____

Test

15 Fosbury Flop Words

blond
moth
trough

hobby
jockey

soccer
sponsor
scholar

hobble
novel
tonsil

hopscotch

problem
common

prophet
profit

column
tropics

baton
adopt

Hear /o/ or /ô/ in every word in the
Fosbury Flop *list.*

We spell /o/ and /ô/ with o.

1. Write the one-syllable words. Underline the word
with two vowel letters and one vowel sound.

2. Write the words with /ər/, /əl/, and /ē/ endings.

_____

_____

3. Write six VCV words. (Do not include **jockey, scholar,** or **novel.**)

_____

_____

4. Write the words with these pronunciations.

   a. /kom′ ən/   **b.** /prob′ ləm/   **c.** /hop′ skoch′/

_____

Working with the Words

1. Write the words with these sounds and spellings.

   a. mn = /m/   **b. gh** = /f/   **c. ph** = /f/

_____

   d. ch = /k/   **e. ch** = /ch/   **f. ck** = /k/

_____

2. Write the synonyms from the list for these words.

   a. gain   **b.** limp   **c.** student

_____

   d. forecaster   **e.** usual   **f.** strange

_____

3. Write the unit words that these pictures suggest.

   a.   **b.**   **c.**

_____

69

blond

moth

trough

hob by

jock ey

soc cer

spon sor

schol ar

hob ble

nov el

ton sil

hop scotch

prob lem

com mon

proph et

prof it

col umn

trop ics

ba ton

a dopt

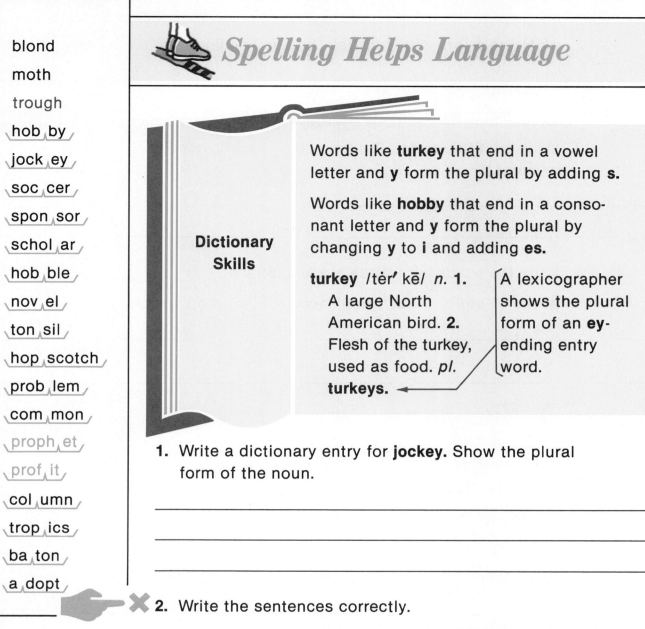

Spelling Helps Language

Dictionary Skills

Words like **turkey** that end in a vowel letter and **y** form the plural by adding **s**.

Words like **hobby** that end in a consonant letter and **y** form the plural by changing **y** to **i** and adding **es**.

turkey /tėr′ kē/ *n.* **1.** A large North American bird. **2.** Flesh of the turkey, used as food. *pl.* **turkeys.**

A lexicographer shows the plural form of an **ey**-ending entry word.

1. Write a dictionary entry for **jockey.** Show the plural form of the noun.

_____

_____

_____

2. Write the sentences correctly.

a. Did the soccer teams have a problem getting a sponser for there games.

_____

_____

b. weather profits in the tropics often forecast humide days.

_____

_____

Look again at the picture on page 68. Explain in a short paragraph what a Fosbury Flop is.

Sound out the /o/ and /ô/ words.

honor	plot	hockey	lobby	topic	doctor
poplar	fossil	topnotch	gossip	logic	proper
throttle	model	snapshot	pollen	modern	foster

You have had enough Dingle Jingles to become an expert jingle solver. Try these.

1. A *swamp jumper* is a _____.

2. A *pale pool* is a _____.

3. *Insect soup* must be _____.

4. An *incorrect bell* is a _____.

5. A *happy streetcar* is a _____.

6. A *well-behaved penny* is a _____.

7. A *warm ink spot* must be a _____.

8. A *short, sturdy horse rider* is a _____.

9. A *correct hatchet* is a _____.

10. A *turkey quarrel* is a _____.

11. A *ten-dime student* is a _____.

12. A *football goalkeeper* is a _____.

13. A *wilted flower* is a _____.

14. *Robert's anteroom* must be _____.

Test

16 Husky Muscle Syllables

sum

bulge

lucky

bulky

sultry

hunger

vulgar

sculptor

S cover

S youngster

muscle

funnel

thumbtack

budget

mustard

custom

adult

result

erupt

mistrust

Hear the /u/ sound in every word in the **Husky Muscle** list.

We spell /u/ with the vowel letter *u*.

1. Write the compound and the one-syllable words. Underline the word with /j/.

2. Write the words with /ər/, /əl/, and /ē/ soft-syllable endings. Note that two words are snurks.

_____

_____

_____

3. Write the words pronounced /ə dult'/, /rē zult'/, /ē rupt'/, and /mis trust'/. Circle the ⌣VC⌣CCV⌣ word.

_____

4. Write the words pronounced /buj' ət/, /mus' tərd/, and /kus' təm/. Underline the word that means "habit."

_____

5. Write the snurks and the word with silent **b**.

_____

Working with the Words

1. Write the adjectives with these meanings.

    a. coarse   **b.** large   **c.** hot and moist

_____

2. Write the picture nouns.

    a.   **b.**   **c.**

_____

3. Write the **ing** forms of the verbs with these meanings.

    a. suspect; doubt   **b.** break out   **c.** swell outward

_____

sum

bulge

luck y

bulk y

sul try

hun ger

vul gar

sculp tor

cov er

young ster

mus cle

fun nel

thumb tack

bud get

mus tard

cus tom

a dult

re sult

e rupt

mis trust

4. Write sentences about a family of three grown-ups and four children who planned how to spend their money to pay for a trip. Use these words: **adults, youngsters, result,** and **budget.**

_____

_____

_____

5. Write sentences about an artist who plans to sell large pieces of sculpture for a lot of money. Use these words: **sum, some, bulky,** and **sculptor.**

_____

_____

_____

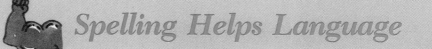 *Spelling Helps Language*

1. We change **y** to **i** before adding **er** and **est** to adjectives like **bulky.** Write the **er** forms of **lucky** and **funny** and the **est** form of **hungry.**

_____

2. Write a correct sentence for each phrase.

a. /luk′ ē əst/ /yung′ stər/

_____

b. /sul′ trē əst/ /weŦH′ ər/

_____

 That's your teammate in the shot-put picture on page 72. Write a note to the editor of your school paper about the picture. Explain what happened.

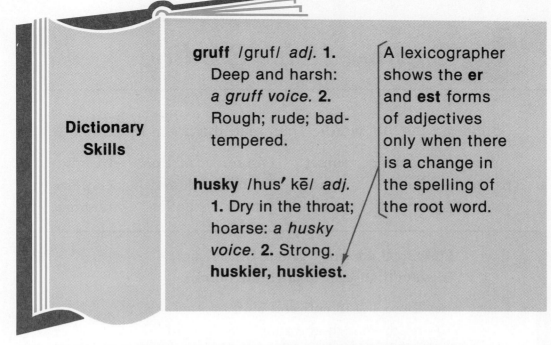

Dictionary Skills

gruff /gruf/ *adj.* **1.** Deep and harsh: *a gruff voice.* **2.** Rough; rude; bad-tempered.

husky /hus′ kē/ *adj.* **1.** Dry in the throat; hoarse: *a husky voice.* **2.** Strong. **huskier, huskiest.**

A lexicographer shows the **er** and **est** forms of adjectives only when there is a change in the spelling of the root word.

3. Write dictionary entries for **sultry** and **bulky.** Write the entries in the order they come in the dictionary. Show the **er** and **est** forms of words. Compare your work with the entries in the Spelling Dictionary.

_____

_____

_____

_____

4. Join syllables from Box A with syllables from Box B to form words with /u/ in the accented syllable. Use each syllable only one time.

A. gul	sum	tun
but	rum	pub
trum		pun

B. pet	ly	nel
ler	lic	ble
ish		mer

_____

_____

Dingle Jingle

If an **amazing error** is a "wonder blunder," what's a **modest mistake?**

_____

Sound out the /u/ words. Then read the poem by parts.

gully	blunder	sunset	custard	mutton	druggist
trumpet	tunnel	bundle	knuckle	rumble	sculpture
summon	summit	public	punish	butler	substance

Boy: "Folks spell an /u/," grunts Uncle Lum,
"In ways that seem to me quite dumb.

Girls: They'll use a **U** in **cuff** and **bluff**.
Who needs **enough** and **rough** and **tough?**
Our spelling would be lots more fun
Without **one, done, come, son,** and **ton.**
And we don't think it's very funny,
Not using **U** in **some** and **money.**
If **U** will do in words like **bubble,**
O-U just gives us **double trouble.**

Boys: And **dove?** and **glove?** and **shove? above?**
Or **month?** and **tongue?** and **young?** and **love?**
There's **southern, done,** and **from** and **blood,**
Among and **couple, honey, flood.**
Why not a **U** in **smother? covers?**"

Girl: My Uncle Lum has lots of **others.**
He's got a list that numbers **dozens,**
All spelled correctly by my **cousins,**
Who all (six sisters and one **brother**),
Take spelling lessons from—their **mother.**

Test

76

17 Spray Waves Syllables

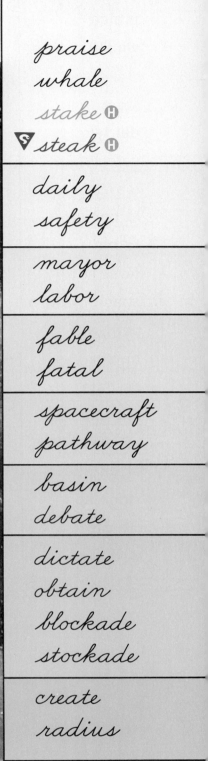

praise
whale
stake Ⓗ
▽ steak Ⓗ

daily
safety

mayor
labor

fable
fatal

spacecraft
pathway

basin
debate

dictate
obtain
blockade
stockade

create
radius

We hear the /ā/ sound in every word in the Spray Waves list.

We spell /ā/ with *ai*, *ay*, and *a* -consonant- *e* .

We use *a* at the end of "open" syllables, as in ‿ba‿sin‿.

 1. Write the words that end with /ər/, /əl/, and /ē/. Underline the adjective that means "every day."

_____

_____

praise

whale

stake

steak

dai ly

safe ty

may or

la bor

fa ble

fa tal

space craft

path way

ba sin

de bate

dic tate

ob tain

block ade

stock ade

cre ate

ra di us

2. Write the ⌄VC⌄CV⌄ and ⌄VCC⌄V⌄ words.

_____

3. Write the compounds. Underline the /ā/ syllables.

_____

4. Write the one-syllable and ⌄V⌄V⌄ words.

_____

_____

5. Write the words that are pronounced /bā′ sən/, /stāk/, and /dik′ tāt/.

_____

Working with the Words

1. Write a spelling word or its plural form for each of these clues.

   a. It went to the moon. _____

   b. It is a huge mammal. _____

   c. It teaches a lesson. _____

   d. The pioneers built them. _____

   e. It has the shape of a bowl. _____

   f. It means "make; cause to be." _____

   g. It means "day by day." _____

   h. It leads from place to place. _____

   i. It gives both sides of a question. _____

Dingle Jingle

If **tie up the dog** is "chain the Great Dane," what is **arouse the serpent?**

_____

 **2.** Write the sentences correctly. Proofread your work.

    a. the people could not /əb tān′/ goods with /sāf′ tē/ because /ᴛнãr/ ships were /blok ād′ əd/

_____

_____

    b. mr blake /dik′ tāts/ /tü/ math problem /dā′ lē/

_____

_____

Spelling Helps Language

Dictionary Skills

stadium /stā′ dē əm/ *n.* Place shaped like an oval or a U with seats around an open field. *pl.* **stadiums** or **stadia.**

A lexicographer shows both forms if a word has two plurals.

1. Write a dictionary entry for **radius.** Write a sentence or phrase to show its meaning. Show two plural forms.

_____

_____

_____

2. Join syllables from Box A with syllables from Box B to write more /ā/ words.

| **A.** la   ba   es   land | **B.** con   dy   scape   tate |

Write a paragraph of explanation to be used under the picture on page 77, which is to appear on your favorite sports page. (Look up **Kayak Racing.**)

Sound out the /ā/ words.

sway	wage	traces	baker	tailor	trailer
naval	cable	lazy	haystack	detail	delay
mason	await	bacon	maintain	estate	contain

✗ Proofread Nicholas Knitpicker's letter and count his mistakes as you did in Unit 11. Write a reply to him.

Dear Editor:

Maybe my last letter did contain a few misstakes. Thats no disgrace and I'm not ashame. I am a Faithful Reader of you're school paper. I have some major complaints about some amazing mistakes I located in your last quiz.

It stated that a razor and one blade cost $1.10. The razor cost a dollar more than the blade. How much did each cost. The razor cost a dollar and the blade cost 10¢.

Your quiz stated, "There is three errers in this sentence. Can you find them?" I know their is only two.

Are you to lazy to create harder problems for we smart students?

Nicholas Knitpicker

How many mistakes?

S _____   P _____   C _____   E _____   F _____

Test

18 Speedy Wheels Words

cheat
sleet
treaty
eager
meter
measles
legal
evil
teammate
freeway
freedom
reason
beneath
deceive
succeed
appeal
between
supreme
mistreat
increase

We hear the /ē/ sound in every word in the **Speedy Wheels** list.

We spell /ē/ with *ee*, *ea*, and *e*-consonant-*e*.

We use *e* in "open" syllables, as in ⌄me⌄ter. We use *y* in final unaccented syllables, as in ⌄treat⌄y.

 1. Write the words in which **ee** spells /ē/. Underline the preposition.

_____

_____

cheat
sleet
treat y
ea ger
me ter
meas les
le gal
e vil
team mate
free way
free dom
rea son
be neath
de ceive
suc ceed
ap peal
be tween
su preme
mis treat
in crease

2. Write the words in which **ea** spells /ē/.

_____

_____

_____

3. Write the words in which **e** spells /ē/.

_____

4. Write the word that ends with **e**-consonant-**e** and the word that ends with /ē/.

_____

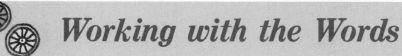

Working with the Words

1. Write the antonyms from the spelling list.

   a. good   **b.** fail   **c.** above

_____

2. Write the synonyms from the spelling list.

   a. fool   **b.** highest   **c.** hurt

_____

   d. beg   **e.** lawful   **f.** agreement

_____

3. Supreme is capitalized when it is used to name the highest court in the United States, the Supreme Court. Write a sentence using the words /sə prēm´/, /kôrt/, and /lē´gəl/.

_____

Dingle Jingle

If a **lawful bird** is a "legal eagle," what's a **lordly hound?**

_____

Spelling Helps Language

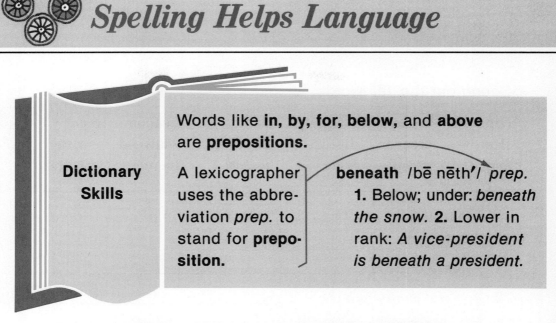

Dictionary Skills

Words like **in, by, for, below,** and **above** are **prepositions.**

A lexicographer uses the abbreviation *prep.* to stand for **preposition.**

beneath /bē nēth′/ *prep.* **1.** Below; under: *beneath the snow.* **2.** Lower in rank: *A vice-president is beneath a president.*

1. Write a dictionary entry for the preposition **between.** Show at least two meanings. Use sentences or phrases to help show the meanings. Compare your entry with the entry in the Spelling Dictionary.

_____

_____

_____

_____

✗ 2. Find the mistakes in these sentences. Write the sentences correctly and underline the three /ē/ snurks.

I believe I have been decieved, I have not received a single copy of the dailey paper

_____

_____

_____

Write a short paragraph on the two kinds of bike racing. What kind is shown in the picture on page 81? Check your facts in an encyclopedia.

Sound out the /ē/ words.

concrete	agree	stampede	demon	beacon	bleat
fleet	treason	disease	daydream	seaweed	weasel
sequel	steeple	fever	feeble	beaver	speedy

An **ocean insect** is a "sea bee." Here are some more Dingle Jingles for you to try.

1. A *main gripe* is a _____.

2. A *metal snaky fish* is a _____.

3. *Colored pants* must be _____.

4. A *low-cost lamb* is a _____.

5. A *cold hug* is a _____.

6. A *puny Athenian* is a _____.

7. A *high jump* is a _____.

8. A *genuine rat* is a _____.

9. A *breakfast agreement* is a _____.

10. A *wicked cotton-eater* is a _____.

11. A *lawyer bird* is a _____.

12. A *best football group* is a _____.

13. A *skinny ruler* is a _____.

14. An *insect's leg joints* are _____.

Test

19 Fly High Words

We hear the /ī/ sound in every word in the **Fly High** list.

We spell /ī/ with *y*, *igh*, and *i* -consonant- *e* .

We use *i* in "open" syllables, as in <u>fi nal</u> .

pry
crime
plight
▽ *height*

ninety

miser
liar
minor

title
final
idol Ⓗ
idle Ⓗ

likewise
typewriter

nylon
deny
crisis

entire
collide
survive

1. Write the four words in which **y** spells /ī/. Underline the words that end with /ī/.

pry

crime

plight

height

nine ty

mi ser

li ar

mi nor

ti tle

fi nal

i dol

i dle

like wise

type wri ter

ny lon

de ny

cri sis

en tire

col lide

sur vive

2. Write the two-syllable words that end with /ər/ or /əl/. Circle the antonym of **major.**

_____

_____

3. Write the words that end in **i**-consonant-**e.** Underline the compound word.

_____

_____

4. Write the words pronounced /plīt/, /hīt/, /krī′ səs/, and /nīn′ tē/. Circle the snurk.

_____

5. Write the pair of homonyms in the list. Circle the antonym of **busy.**

_____

Working with the Words

1. Write the words with these meanings.

   a. less important   **b.** time of danger   **c.** complete

_____

2. Write the picture verbs from the spelling list. Beneath each word write its **ed** form.

   a.   **b.**   **c.**

_____

3. Unscramble the underlined words to form a sentence. Correct punctuation and capitalization mistakes.

"The <u>survived</u> <u>miser</u> <u>an</u> for <u>winter</u> <u>entire</u> <u>on</u> <u>dollars</u> <u>ninety</u> explained mike.

_____

_____

Spelling Helps Language

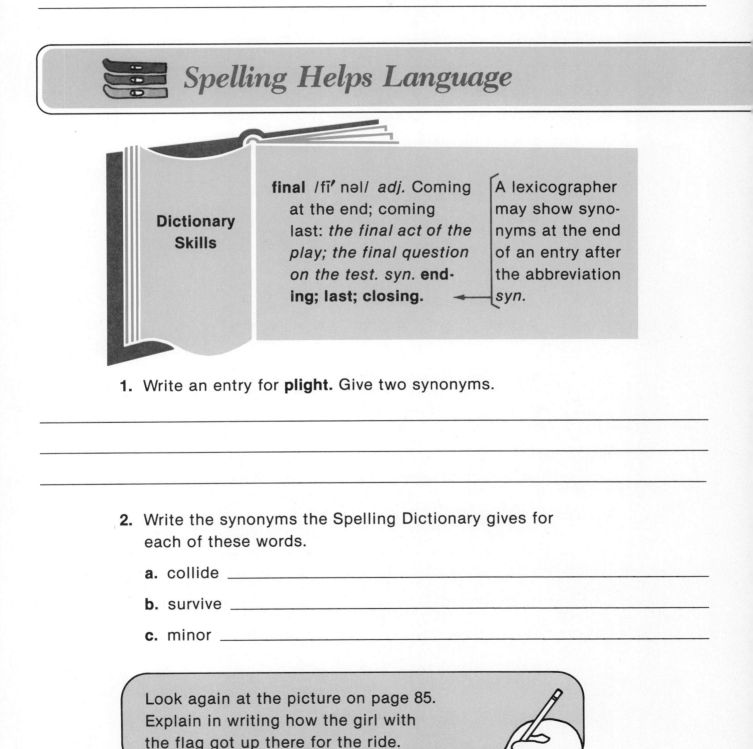

Dictionary Skills

final /fī′ nəl/ *adj.* Coming at the end; coming last: *the final act of the play; the final question on the test.* syn. **ending; last; closing.**

A lexicographer may show synonyms at the end of an entry after the abbreviation *syn.*

1. Write an entry for **plight.** Give two synonyms.

_____

_____

_____

2. Write the synonyms the Spelling Dictionary gives for each of these words.

a. collide _____

b. survive _____

c. minor _____

> Look again at the picture on page 85. Explain in writing how the girl with the flag got up there for the ride.

Sound out the /ī/ words. Then complete the sentences.

termite	nigh	style	hyphen	bison	rifle
umpire	alive	lilac	spice	visor	desire
climate	shy	beside	tidy	rival	pipeline

1. **Nine** is to **ninety** as a **dime** is to a...
       a. penny   **b.** dollar   **c.** nickel

2. **Like** is to **hate** as **admire** is to...
       a. oblige   **b.** surprise   **c.** despise

3. **Spike** is to **tack** as **major** is to...
       a. minor   **b.** microbe   **c.** pilot

4. **Smile** is to **glare** as **ally** is to...
       a. friend   **b.** sky   **c.** rival

5. **Violet** is to **flower** as **cypress** is to...
       a. pine   **b.** tree   **c.** vine

6. **Private** is to **public** as **inside** is to...
       a. outside   **b.** offside   **c.** skyline

7. **Termite** is to **insect** as **crocodile** is to...
       a. mammal   **b.** tiger   **c.** reptile

Dingle Jingle

If the **name of an important book** is a "vital title," what's a **whole chorus?**

_____

Test

20 Polo Solo Syllables

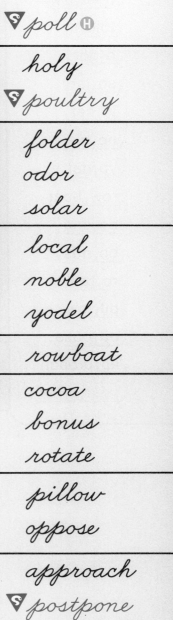

boast
growth
clothes
⬦ poll

holy
▽ poultry

folder
odor
solar

local
noble
yodel

rowboat

cocoa
bonus
rotate

pillow
oppose

approach
▽ postpone

We hear the /ō/ sound in every word in the **Polo Solo** list.

We spell /ō/ with *oa*, *ow*, *o(ld)*, and *o*-consonant-*e*.

We use *o* in "open" syllables, as in ˎso ˏlar ˎ.

1. Write the four /ō/ words with **ow** or **o(ld)**. Underline the one-syllable word.

boast
growth
clothes
poll
ho·ly
poul·try
fold·er
o·dor
so·lar
lo·cal
no·ble
yo·del
row·boat
co·coa
bo·nus
ro·tate
pil·low
op·pose
ap·proach
post·pone

2. Write **clothes** and the words ending in **o-consonant-e.** Underline the word that means "go against."

_____

3. Write the words in which **oa** spells /ō/.

_____

4. Write **holy** and the **er** and **est** forms of **holy.**

_____

5. Write the unit word for each pronunciation. Underline each snurk spelling of /ō/.

    a. /pōl′ trē/   **b.** /ō′ dər/   **c.** /yō′ dəl/

_____

    d. /nō′ bəl/   **e.** /pōl/   **f.** /lō′ kəl/

_____

    g. /rō′ tāt/   **h.** /bō′ nəs/   **i.** /sō′ lər/

_____

Working with the Words

1. Join syllables from Box A with syllables from Box B to form spelling words. Write the words.

A.	pil	lo	co
	op	no	ho

B.	low	ly	cal
		pose	coa	ble

_____

2. Write the spelling words these pictures suggest.

a. _____

b. _____

3. Write the words for these meanings.

    a. put off   **b.** come near   **c.** brag

    d. turn   **e.** take votes   **f.** smell

4. Write the picture words. Underline the noun for which there is no singular form.

    a.   **b.**   **c.**

5. Write the **ing** forms of the words **oppose, postpone, rotate, yodel,** and **poll.**

6. Unscramble the underlined words to form sentences. Correct all spelling mistakes.

    a. I hope that <u>local</u> <u>the</u> <u>store</u> <u>postpone</u> <u>it's</u> <u>won't</u> <u>of</u> <u>pillow</u> <u>sail</u>.

    b. No <u>a</u> <u>one</u> <u>bonus</u> <u>geting</u> <u>opposes</u>.

    c. Of <u>heat</u> <u>gives</u> <u>coarse</u> <u>solar</u> <u>sun</u> <u>the</u>.

Look again at the picture on page 89.
Explain briefly what handicaps are in
polo and how they affect scoring.

Dictionary Skills

noble /nō′ bəl/ *adj.*
Excellent; fine: *a noble deed; a noble person.*
nobler, noblest. ◄——

A lexicographer shows **er** and **est** forms when the spelling changes before the endings are added.

1. Write a dictionary entry for the word **holy.** Show the **er** and **est** forms.

_____

_____

2. Write one sentence using **clothe** and another sentence using **clothes.** Check the word meanings.

_____

_____

3. Write one sentence using both **poll** and **pole.**

_____

4. The **er** is the "more," or **comparative,** form of an adjective. The **est** is the "most," or **superlative,** form. Write the superlative forms of these adjectives.

   a. noble   **b.** narrow   **c.** bold

   _____

   d. coarse   **e.** mellow   **f.** cold

   _____

Dingle Jingle

If **your own clumsy fellow** is a "local yokel," what's a **filing cabinet?**

_____

Sound out the /ō/ words. Then read the poem by parts.

coax	owner	clover	polar	over	focus
blown	rainbow	narrow	nomad	bellow	total
quote	charcoal	donate	cargo	suppose	poet

Oval O

Boy: Without you we could not say, "No!"
You roly-poly, oval **O**.
You're both a letter and a zero
(And, in Ohio, quite a hero).

Girl: You're seen in frozen polar zones,
In soda, cokes, and ice cream cones.
You'll sing a local vocal solo
And ride your pony playing polo.

All: Without you we can do no boasting,
Soaking, croaking, toasting, coasting,

Boy: Sleep on pillows, play at lotto,
Write a poem—or a motto.

Girl: You ride on bronchos, throw a lasso
From Amarillo—to El Paso,

All: Play piano, strum the cello.
Oval **O**, you're quite a fellow!

Test

21 Super Crew Words

tube
brew
flue ⒣
cruise ⒣

screwdriver

truly

rumor

sewer

lunar

jewel

brutal

bugle

▽ neutral

usual

manual

duet

tulip

cubic

perfume

issue

We hear /ū/ or /ü/ in every word in the **Super Crew** list.

We spell /ū/ or /ü/ with *ew*, *ui*, *ue*, and *u*-consonant-*e*.

We use *u* at the end of "open" syllables, as in ⌐ru⌐mor⌐.

1. Write the words with the VV syllabic pattern. Circle the word that means "done with the hands."

2. Write the compound and the two-syllable words that end with /ər/ or /əl/. Circle the compound.

_____

_____

3. Write the words in which **ue** or **u**-consonant-**e** spells /ü/. Circle the word that means "a passage for hot air."

_____

4. There are ten spelling words in which **u** spells /ū/ or /ü/ at the end of an "open" syllable. Write the five that are used as adjectives.

_____

5. Write the words with these pronunciations.

    a. /tü′ lip/   **b.** /krüz/   **c.** /nü′ trəl/

_____

    d. /trü′ lē/   **e.** /brü/   **f.** /kū′ bik/

_____

Working with the Words

1. Write the picture words.

    a.   **b.**   **c.**

_____

    d.   **e.**   **f.**

_____

tube

brew

flue

cruise

screw driv er

tru ly

ru mor

sew er

lu nar

jew el

bru tal

bu gle

neu tral

u su al

man u al

du et

tu lip

cu bic

per fume

is sue

2. Write an antonym from the list for each word.

    a. gentle   **b.** fact   **c.** receive

_____

3. Write the sentence, using spelling words to fill the spaces. Note that a comma is used to separate the phrase at the beginning from the rest of the sentence.

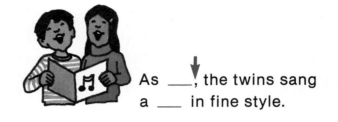

As ___, the twins sang a ___ in fine style.

_____

_____

4. Write the sentence, using **ing** and plural forms of spelling words. Note that commas are used between words in a series.

Mr. Bruce is ___ drums, flutes, and ___ to the band.

_____

_____

5. Write the sentence, using plural forms of spelling words. Note that commas are used around the words that explain another word.

The chimney has two ___, or ___, through which the smoke may pass.

_____

_____

Spelling Helps Language

Dictionary Skills

An **adverb** tells **when, where,** or **how.**

surely /shúr′ lē/ *adv.*
1. Certainly: *We surely miss you.* 2. Without mistake: *The goat leaped surely to the rock.*

The abbreviation *adv.* stands for **adverb.**

1. Write a dictionary entry for the adverb **truly,** using a phrase to show meaning.

_____

_____

_____

2. Write a sentence using **flew** and another using its homonym **flue.** Use the Spelling Dictionary.

_____

_____

3. Write a question using the word **crews** and another using its homonym **cruise.** Use the Spelling Dictionary.

_____

_____

4. Write one sentence in which you use the snurk **neutral** and the word **rumor.**

_____

Explain what is happening in the **Super Crew** rowing photograph on page 94. (Look up **Rowing** in your encyclopedia for information.)

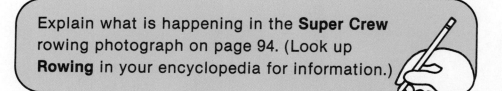

97

Sound out the /ū/ and /ü/ words. Then write the rhymes.

fuse	duel	fume	fluid	chew	newscast
ruby	super	juicy	cruel	salute	unit
abuse	tissue	assume	brewer	humor	glue

A **silent beast** is a "mute brute." Here are some more Dingle Jingles for you to try.

1. A *pretty outfit* is a _____.

2. A *clever fellow* is a _____.

3. A *correct hint* must be a _____.

4. A *recent church bench* is a _____.

5. A *faithful color* must be _____.

6. A *summer melody* is a _____.

7. A *wise pupil* must be a _____.

8. An *unkind fight* is a _____.

9. *Give out Kleenex* means _____.

10. *Funny gossip* must be _____.

11. *Colored sticking fluid* is _____.

12. A *yearly instruction book* is an _____.

13. *Susan's information* is _____.

14. A *moon snipper* must be a _____.

Test

22 Rooftop Loop Syllables

proof
moor
whoop
flood

gloomy
wooly

rooster
cooker

cookbook
rooftop
toothache

igloo
bamboo
shampoo
harpoon
cartoon

wooden
foolish

maroon
cocoon

We hear /u̇/ or /ü/ in every word in the **Rooftop Loop** list except the snurk.

We spell /u̇/ and /ü/ with *oo*.

1. Write the one-syllable words and the compounds. Underline each /ü/ spelling.

proof
moor
whoop
flood
gloom y
wool y
roost er
cook er
cook book
roof top
tooth ache
ig loo
bam boo
sham poo
har poon
car toon
wood en
fool ish
ma roon
co coon

2. Write the words with an accent on the second syllable only. Use the Spelling Dictionary.

_____

_____

3. Write the words with an accented first syllable and an unaccented second syllable.

_____

_____

4. Write the words pronounced /flud/, /hüp/, and /mur/. Underline the homonym of **hoop.**

_____

② Working with the Words

1. Write the words that complete the sentences.

   a. A loud cry is a _____.

   b. Very dark red is the color _____.

   c. One who is not wise is _____.

   d. A dark and dreary day is _____.

   e. A barnyard fowl is a _____.

   f. We wash our hair with _____.

   g. An "ice house" is an _____.

   h. Heather grows on a _____.

Dingle Jingle

If **Lulu's hints** are "Lu's clues," what are **Susan's slippers?**

_____

2. Write a sentence or two explaining the difference between a **carton** and a **cartoon.** Proofread your work.

_____

_____

Spelling Helps Language

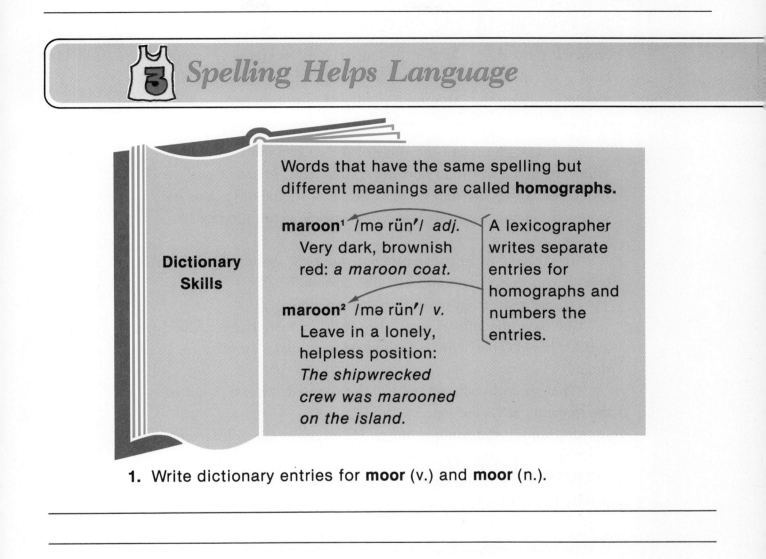

Dictionary Skills

Words that have the same spelling but different meanings are called **homographs.**

maroon¹ /mə rün′/ *adj.* Very dark, brownish red: *a maroon coat.*

maroon² /mə rün′/ *v.* Leave in a lonely, helpless position: *The shipwrecked crew was marooned on the island.*

A lexicographer writes separate entries for homographs and numbers the entries.

1. Write dictionary entries for **moor** (v.) and **moor** (n.).

_____

_____

_____

_____

2. Write the missing spelling words. (One word needs **ed.**)

They were ___ on their ___ during the ___!

_____

In a few sentences, write what is happening in the basketball picture on page 99.

Sound out the /u̇/ and /ü/ words. Then read the story.

crooked	hood	hoofer	lagoon	booklet	scoop
hoof	moody	poodle	baboon	footstool	balloon
moose	booster	trooper	loophole	mushroom	shook

Of course you recall the story of the foolish old man who killed the goose that had laid the golden eggs. When it was found that the goose had no gold inside of it, the old man's wife stamped her foot and shook her broomstick at her gloomy husband.

"You'll have us in the poorhouse, booby!" she cried. "I ought to lock you up in the woodshed like a schoolboy!"

The old man tried to sooth his angry wife.

"We have the golden eggs," he said. "In fact, Banker Moody and his bookkeeper will be here at noon to make an offer for them."

"That smooth-talking crook?" she shouted. "If we're not on the lookout, he'll steal our rooftop!"

Mr. Moody did come at noon. He weighed the golden eggs.

"Choose, good folks," he said. "I'll give you a cool $1,000,000.00 for the eggs, or I'll give you a penny today and double the amount each day thereafter for thirty days."

Which offer should the old man and his wife choose? How much would they get if they chose the second offer?

Test

23 Trout Crowd Syllables

bound
vow
▽ tour
▽ tough

grouchy
rowdy
drowsy

vowel
counsel ℍ
council ℍ

counter
shower

countdown
playground

allow
account
surround

coward

arouse
trousers

> We hear /ou/ in every word in the
> Trout Crowd list except the snurks.
>
> We spell /ou/ with *ou* or *ow*.

 1. Write the one-syllable words and the compounds.
Underline each /ou/ spelling. Circle the snurks.

_____

_____

bound

vow

tour

tough

grouch‿y

row‿dy

drow‿sy

vow‿el

coun‿sel

coun‿cil

count‿er

show‿er

count‿down

play‿ground

al‿low

ac‿count

sur‿round

cow‿ard

a‿rouse

trou‿sers

2. Write the words that end in /ər/, /əl/, or /ē/.

_____

_____

3. Write the three words that are divided between doubled consonants.

_____

4. Write the words pronounced /trou′zərz/, /ə rouz′/, and /kou′ərd/. Underline the word that is divided between two vowel *sounds*.

_____

🐟 *Working with the Words*

1. Write **counsel** and **council** and the **ed** and the **ing** forms of the one that may be used as a verb. Use the Spelling Dictionary.

_____

2. Write the **er** and **est** forms of the three adjectives that end with **y.**

_____

_____

3. Write the missing /ou/ spelling words.

Students will be ___ to

accept the wise ___ of

the Student Council.

_____

Dingle Jingle

If **stir up the Hereford** is "arouse the cow," what's **surprise the dog?**

_____

Spelling Helps Language

Some nouns have no singular form.

A lexicographer uses *pl.* to show plural nouns. ⟶ **outskirts** /out′ skėrts′/ *n. pl.* Outer parts or edges of a town: *a farm on the outskirts of Rockford.*

1. Write a dictionary entry for the plural noun **trousers.** Give at least one sample sentence.

_____

_____

_____

2. Write the sentences using spelling words to fill the spaces. Correct spelling and punctuation mistakes.

a. As usuel the ___ will ___ no ___ gatherings on the ___.

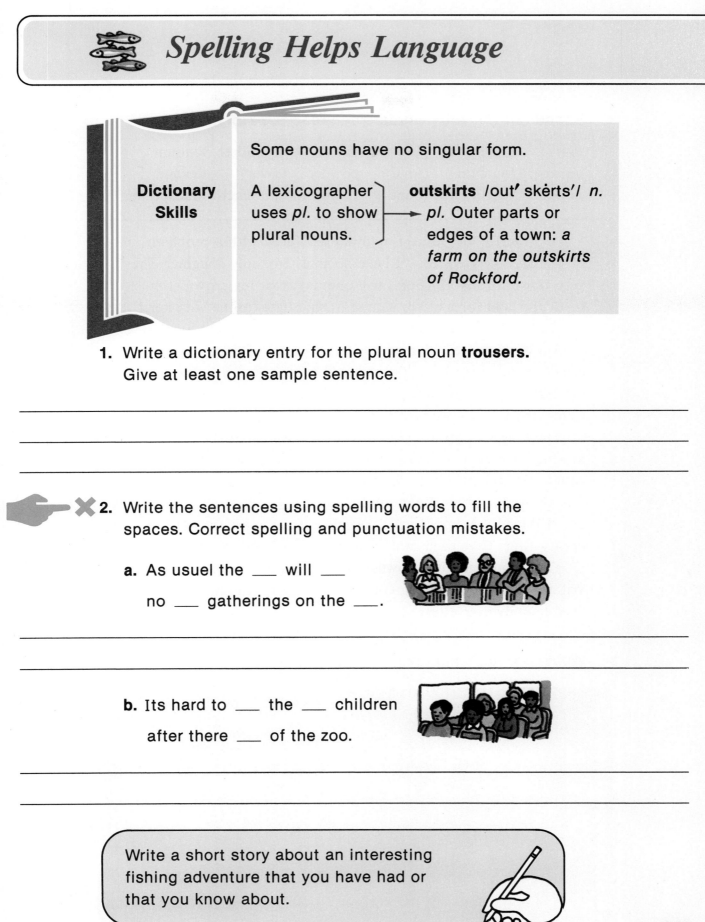

_____

_____

b. Its hard to ___ the ___ children after there ___ of the zoo.

_____

_____

Write a short story about an interesting fishing adventure that you have had or that you know about.

Sound out the /ou/ words. Then read the story.

sour	pronounce	pounce	pouch	scoundrel	amount
brown	fountain	cloudy	powder	towel	devour
astound	hound	foundry	flounder	announce	loudspeaker

A powerful king once found himself faced with a problem.

"Alas," he growled, "I have no sons. My only daughter, the very flower of my kingdom, will one day wear my crown. I must scour the land for a clever spouse to share the throne with her."

And so the proud king announced a contest for her hand.

The king spoke, "A man has left his herd of twenty-three camels to his three sons. The eldest gets half the herd. The second son gets one-third, and the last one-eighth. How can we follow the father's wishes?"

The king was soon surrounded by thousands of shouting, howling men eager to marry the princess. But, alas, not one could solve the problem. At last a poor lad in baggy trousers was allowed to enter the grounds.

"I'll lend you my camel," he said, "to increase the herd to twenty-four. Give each son his share. Then return my camel."

The astounded king frowned and pounded the lad's back. Within the hour the young couple made their wedding vows and lived happily ever after.

Would the lad's plan work? Why or why not?

106

24 Poise Pointer Syllables

We hear /oi/ in every word in the **Poise Pointer** list except the snurk.

We spell /oi/ with *oi* or *oy*.

poise
void
▽ choir

pointless
boyhood
loyal
royal

oyster
loiter
pointer

annoy
alloy
appoint
moisten

rejoice
boycott
decoy
moisture

embroider
employer

1. Write the compounds and the one-syllable words. Circle the snurk.

_____

_____

poise
void
choir
point less
boy hood
loy al
roy al
oy ster
loi ter
point er
an noy
al loy
ap point
mois ten
re joice
boy cott
de coy
mois ture
em broi der
em ploy er

2. Write the words with the /əl/ or /ər/ soft-syllable ending. Underline the three-syllable words.

_____

_____

3. Write the words that end with the /oi/ sound.

_____

4. Write the words pronounced /boi′ kot/, /mois′ ən/, and /ə point′/. Underline each /oi/ spelling.

_____

5. Write the words with these sounds and spellings.

    a. ch = /k/   **b. ce** = /s/   **c. ture** = /chər/

_____

Working with the Words

1. Write a synonym from the spelling list for the underlined word in each phrase.

    a. an <u>empty</u> space _____

    b. a <u>faithful</u> subject of the king _____

    c. a <u>majestic</u> procession _____

    d. amount of <u>wetness</u> in the air _____

    e. a fine church <u>chorus</u> _____

    f. <u>dampen</u> a piece of cloth _____

    g. <u>balance</u> at the edge _____

    h. <u>bother</u> a person _____

    i. <u>linger</u> along the way _____

    j. <u>select</u> new officers _____

2. Join syllables from Box A with syllables from Box B
to write eight /oi/ words.

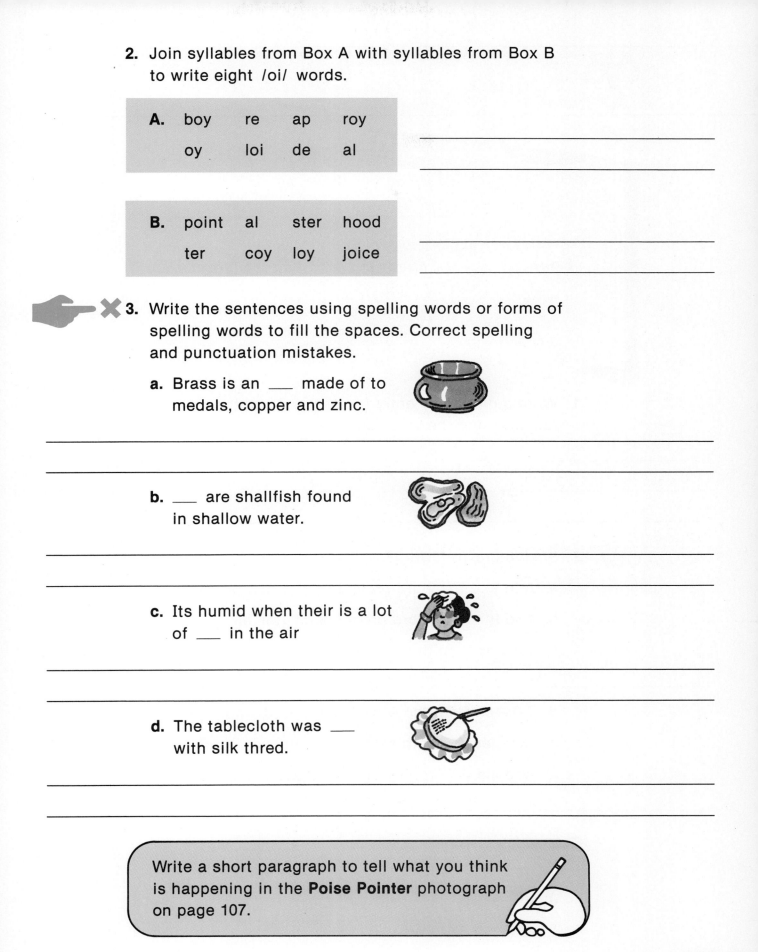

A. boy   re   ap   roy

oy   loi   de   al

_____

_____

B. point   al   ster   hood

ter   coy   loy   joice

_____

_____

3. Write the sentences using spelling words or forms of
spelling words to fill the spaces. Correct spelling
and punctuation mistakes.

a. Brass is an ___ made of to
medals, copper and zinc.

_____

_____

b. ___ are shallfish found
in shallow water.

_____

_____

c. Its humid when their is a lot
of ___ in the air

_____

_____

d. The tablecloth was ___
with silk thred.

_____

_____

Write a short paragraph to tell what you think
is happening in the **Poise Pointer** photograph
on page 107.

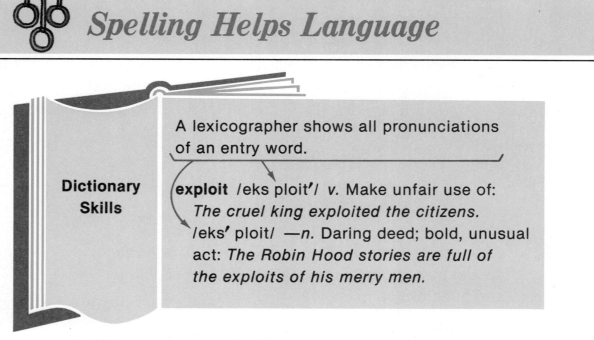

Dictionary Skills

A lexicographer shows all pronunciations of an entry word.

exploit /eks ploit′/ *v.* Make unfair use of: *The cruel king exploited the citizens.* /eks′ ploit/ —*n.* Daring deed; bold, unusual act: *The Robin Hood stories are full of the exploits of his merry men.*

1. Write a dictionary entry for **decoy.** Show the noun /dē′ koi/ and the verb /dē koi′/.

_____

_____

_____

2. Spell more /oi/ words.

   a. Add **y** to the word pronounced /em broi′ dər/.

   b. Add **ly** to the word pronounced /loi′ əl/.

   c. Take **er** from the word pronounced /em ploi′ ər/.

   d. Take **en** from the word pronounced /mois′ ən/.

   e. Take **less** from the word pronounced /point′ ləs/.

   f. Add **ment** to the word pronounced /ə point′/.

Dingle Jingle

If a **plush English car** is a "choice Rolls Royce," what's a **convent for a shellfish?**

_____

Sound out the /oi/ words.

toil	joist	anoint	convoy	broiler	choice
doily	boiler	pinpoint	oilcloth	employ	destroy
coin	poison	voyage	alloy	adjoin	avoid

Proofread Nicholas Knitpicker's letter and count his mistakes as you did in Unit 11. Write a reply to Nicholas explaining his mistakes.

Dear Editor:

I'm not anoyed when you pinpoint the mistakes I make in my letters. We won't avoid making some errors, will we. Appoint me to your staff. Id enjoy working with you.

My cousin Joyce Doyle from Royal Oaks michigan is visiting us. She joins me in pointing out that you have a wrong quiz answer in you're last issue. The quiz states that 5 cats can destroy 5 mice in 5 minutes. Then it asks, "how many cats are needed to destroy 100 mice in 100 minutes." Your answer is 5! I hate to spoil your day. The answer is 100. My choice would be to employ poison if I had mice loitering around.

Your loyal reader,

Nicholas Knitpicker

How many mistakes?

S _____ P _____ C _____ E _____ F _____

Test

gaunt
flaw
waltz

drawbridge
jigsaw

salty
scrawny

saucer
lawyer
alter (H)
(S) laughter

walrus
wallet
walnut
awkward

autumn
faucet

applaud
install
laundry

25 Caught the Saucer Words

We hear /ô/ in every word in the **Caught the Saucer** list except the snurk.

We spell /ô/ with aw, au, and $a(l)$.

1. Write the compounds and the one-syllable words. Underline the word that means "thin and bony."

2. Write the words with **a** before **l**. Circle the word that means "change."

_____

_____

3. Write the **aw** words. Circle the word that means "clumsy."

_____

_____

4. Write the **au** words. Underline the snurk.

_____

_____

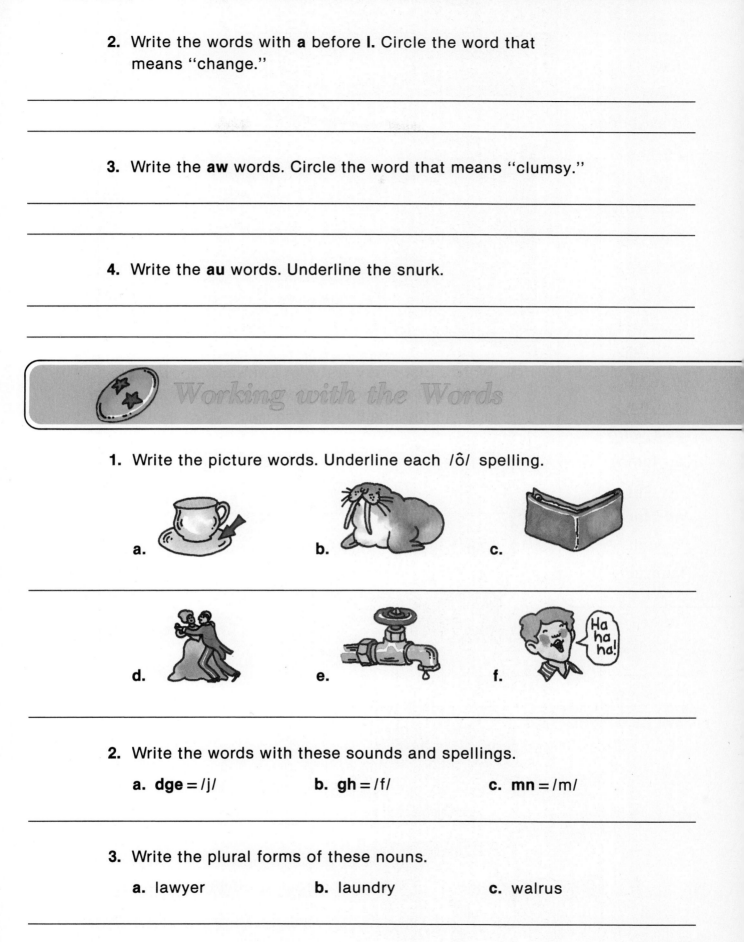

Working with the Words

1. Write the picture words. Underline each /ô/ spelling.

a.

b.

c.

_____

d.

e.

f.

_____

2. Write the words with these sounds and spellings.

   a. dge = /j/   **b. gh** = /f/   **c. mn** = /m/

_____

3. Write the plural forms of these nouns.

   a. lawyer   **b.** laundry   **c.** walrus

gaunt

flaw

waltz

draw bridge

jig saw

salt y

scraw ny

sau cer

law yer

al ter

laugh ter

wal rus

wal let

wal nut

awk ward

au tumn

fau cet

ap plaud

in stall

laun dry

Spelling Helps Language

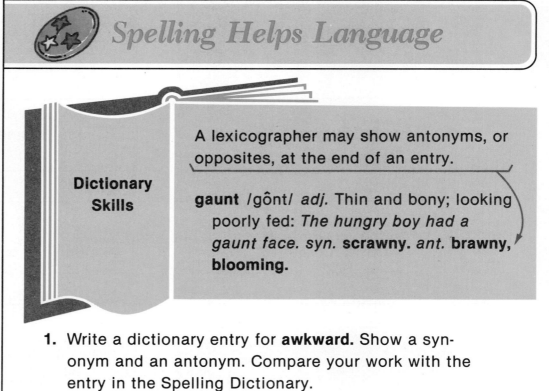

Dictionary Skills

A lexicographer may show antonyms, or opposites, at the end of an entry.

gaunt /gônt/ *adj.* Thin and bony; looking poorly fed: *The hungry boy had a gaunt face. syn.* **scrawny.** *ant.* **brawny, blooming.**

1. Write a dictionary entry for **awkward.** Show a synonym and an antonym. Compare your work with the entry in the Spelling Dictionary.

_____

_____

_____

2. Join syllables from the two boxes to form six more /ô/ words. Write the words.

draw	flaw	daugh
au	pau	sauce

er	burn	less
per	ter	pan

_____

Write a short paragraph telling about the smartest dog trick you ever saw.

Dingle Jingle

If a **dish thrower** is a "saucer tosser," what's **this book publisher's mistakes?**

_____

114

Sound out the /ô/ words.

faultless	auburn	awe	brawny	taught	haul
scald	launch	malt	falter	applause	pauper
sausage	clause	sprawl	awning	crawfish	dawdle

Guess the meanings of the boldface words by the way they are used in the sentences. Choose the correct meanings.

1. We jeered at our brave leader when he did not begin a strong **assault** against the enemy fort.

   plan   retreat   attack

2. We jeered at our brave leader when he did not **launch** an assault against the enemy fort.

   start   delay   plan

3. We **taunted** our brave leader when he did not begin an assault against the enemy fort.

   jeered at   supported   helped

4. We taunted our **dauntless** leader when he did not launch an assault against the enemy fort.

   awkward   foolhardy   fearless

5. We **lauded** our dauntless leader when he did launch an assault against the enemy fort.

   jeered at   praised   blamed

Test

harsh
chart

tardy
parsley
parlor
armor

sparkle
parcel

hardship
bookmark
barbershop

carbon
cargo
margin
target
harvest
scarlet
 sergeant

depart
apart

26 Par Star Syllables

We hear /är/ in every word in the Par Star list.

We spell /är/ with *ar*.

1. Write the words that end with /ē/, /ər/, or /əl/. Underline the word used as an adjective.

2. Write the VCCV words that do not have /ē/, /ər/, or /əl/ endings. Underline each accented syllable.

_____

_____

3. Write the VCV words. Circle the word that means "aside."

_____

4. Write the words in which **g** spells /j/. Circle the snurk.

_____

5. Write the words with either /sh/ or /ch/.

_____

 Working with the Words

1. Write synonyms from the spelling list.

   a. The synonym of **leave** is _____ .

   b. The synonym of **edge** is _____ .

   c. The synonym of **red** is _____ .

   d. The synonym of **late** is _____ .

   e. The synonym of **rough** is _____ .

   f. The synonym of **map** is _____ .

2. Write antonyms from the spelling list.

   a. The antonym of **prompt** is _____ .

   b. The antonym of **together** is _____ .

   c. The antonym of **arrive** is _____ .

   d. The antonym of **ease** is _____ .

   e. The antonym of **kind** is _____ .

   f. The antonym of **plant** is _____ .

3. Unscramble the words to write declarative sentences. Use correct capitalization and punctuation.

a. privates   rank   sergeants
above   the   in   army

_____

_____

b. once   armor   about   pounds
wore   65   weighing   knights

_____

_____

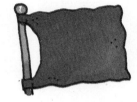

c. is   maroon   color   brighter
scarlet   a   than   not

_____

_____

d. used   is   parsley   flavor
garden   a   food   plant   to

_____

_____

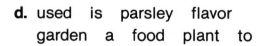 *Spelling Helps Language*

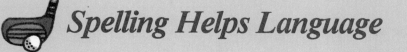 Write a brief definition for each of these golf terms: **par, birdie, eagle,** and **bogey.**

118

Dictionary Skills

Some **o**-ending words form their plurals by adding **s** or **es**.

zero /zir′ ō/ *n.* **1.** The figure or digit 0: *There are two zeros in 100.* **2.** Nothing. *pl.* **zeros** or **zeroes.**

A lexicographer shows both spellings when two plurals are correct.

1. Write a dictionary entry for **cargo**. Show correct plural spellings. Use the plural form of **cargo** in a sample sentence.

_____

_____

_____

2. Join syllables from the two boxes to form /är/ words. Write the words.

arm	car	arc
var	har	war

toon	tic	ble
nish	y	ness

_____

_____

3. Write the picture words from Exercise 2.

a.   b.   c.

_____

Dingle Jingle

If a **pretty milkmaid** is a "farmer charmer," what should a cold knight have?

_____

harsh
chart
tar dy
pars ley
par lor
ar mor
spar kle
par cel
hard ship
book mark
bar ber shop
car bon
car go
mar gin
tar get
har vest
scar let
ser geant
de part
a part

Sound out the /är/ words. Then read the story.

charcoal	party	partner	quarry	marvel	gargle
starve	carve	arctic	charter	carcass	farther
varnish	charm	warden	arbor	jargon	harmless

Miss Brewster's pupils were writing Dingle Jingles. They had to use only /är/ words.

"Now let's not have those far-out word partners that Arthur dreams up," remarked Martha Parker.

"I beg your pardon, Martha," snickered Arthur Carpenter. "You mean I can't use Fargo Cargo?"

"I'll start," said Marvin Carson. "Here's a hard one. Gloomy animal boat."

"Dark ark," cried Charles Martin.

Now guess these other Dingle Jingles.

1. two clever pints

_____

2. hot beehive family

_____

3. Charles's grain

_____

4. dock garment

_____

5. plant watchman

_____

6. metal suit heater

_____

7. hot signal

_____

8. shopping wagon

_____

9. bird bullet

_____

10. Cupid's arrow

_____

 *Test*

27 Formal Horse Syllables

form
lore
▽ source
coarse Ⓗ
hoarse Ⓗ

seaport
forearm

normal
oral
moral
morsel

porter
former
horror
mortar

absorb
ignore
assort
torment
borrow

We hear /ôr/ in every word in the **Formal Horse** list.

We spell /ôr/ with *or*, *ore*, and *oar*.

1. Write the one-syllable words. Circle the snurk.

_____

_____

form
lore
source
coarse
hoarse
sea‚port‚
fore‚arm‚
nor‚mal‚
or‚al‚
mor‚al‚
mor‚sel‚
por‚ter‚
form‚er‚
hor‚ror‚
mor‚tar‚
ab‚sorb‚
ig‚nore‚
as‚sort‚
tor‚ment‚
bor‚row‚

2. Write the compounds.

_____

3. Write the three VCCV words that are always accented on the second syllable.

_____

4. Write the /ər/ and /əl/ words. Underline the word that means "tiny piece."

_____

_____

5. Write the homonym of **horse** and the antonym of **lend.**

_____

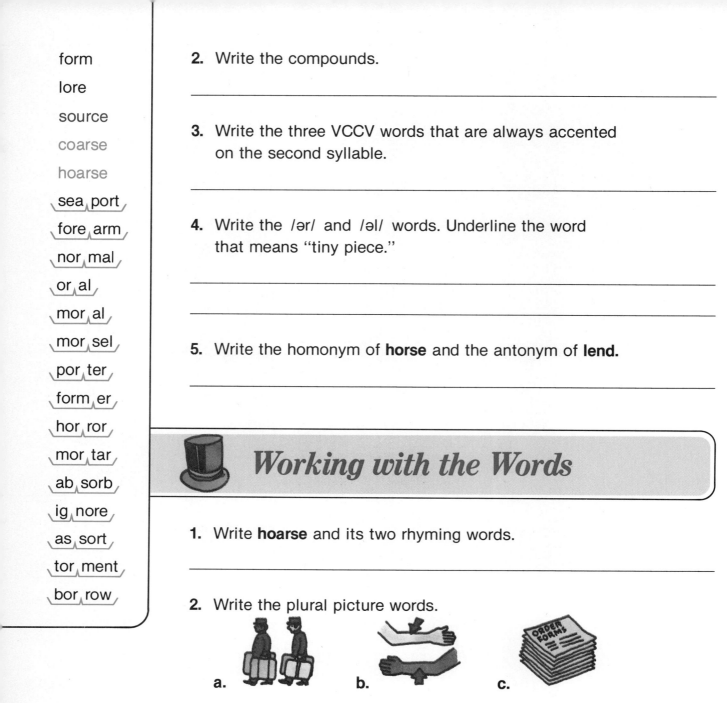

Working with the Words

1. Write **hoarse** and its two rhyming words.

_____

2. Write the plural picture words.

a. _____   b. _____   c. _____

3. Write the spelling words for these meanings.

   a. tiny piece   **b.** annoy   **c.** facts and stories

Dingle Jingle

If **spoken wisdom** is an "oral moral," what's a **smaller baggage carrier?**

_____

Spelling Helps Language

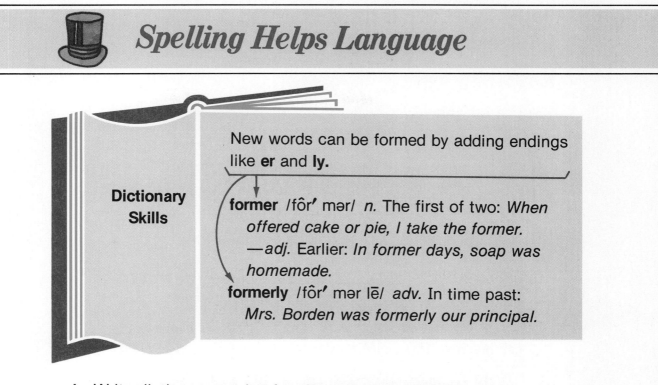

Dictionary Skills

New words can be formed by adding endings like **er** and **ly**.

former /fôr′ mər/ *n.* The first of two: *When offered cake or pie, I take the former.* —*adj.* Earlier: *In former days, soap was homemade.*

formerly /fôr′ mər lē/ *adv.* In time past: *Mrs. Borden was formerly our principal.*

1. Write dictionary entries for **absorb** and **absorbing.**

_____

_____

_____

_____

2. Write the sentences correctly.

a. of coarse, work clothes are often made of course cloth, I said in a horse voice.

_____

_____

b. many absorbing horrer tails are part of our folklore.

_____

_____

Explain in a short paragraph what the difference is between a horse's gallop and a horse's trot.

Sound out the /ôr/ words.

score	orchard	forecast	torrent	chorus	pore
glory	adore	forest	forlorn	chord	forge
roar	oriole	hornet	formal	sorry	fort

Explain the meaning of the boldface expressions.

1. **"Any port in a storm,"** cried Nora, as she dived under our porch when an angry hornet came buzzing at her.

2. **"Look before you leap,"** said Mrs. Horton, as Flora poured her hot breakfast coffee over her cornflakes.

3. **"There are more ways than one to skin a cat,"** said Gloria, as she paddled the boat ashore with a broken board.

4. **"Forewarned is forearmed,"** snorted Mr. Norton hoarsely, as he turned off the newscast and put on his raincoat.

5. **"Great oaks from little acorns grow,"** said Mr. Norman, as his young son tore around the bases to score a run.

6. It was Little Jack Horner sitting in a corner who was **blowing his own horn,** not Little Boy Blue.

7. **"Hold your horses!"** roared Mother. "We can't afford forty or fifty boxes of popcorn from the corner store."

Test

28 Sturdy Hurdle Words

nerve
thirst
burst

outburst
furthermore

jersey
mercy
sturdy

hurdle
colonel H
kernel H

burner
murder

fertile
permit
service
person
pursue
surface
furnish

We hear /ėr/ in every word in the **Sturdy Hurdle** list.

We spell /ėr/ with *er*, *ur*, and *ir*.

1. Write the words with /ər/ and /ē/ endings and the words in which **le** or **el** spells /əl/.

_____

_____

nerve

thirst

burst

out‚burst

fur‚ther‚more

jer‚sey

mer‚cy

stur‚dy

hur‚dle

col‚on‚el

ker‚nel

burn‚er

mur‚der

fer‚tile

per‚mit

ser‚vice

per‚son

pur‚sue

sur‚face

fur‚nish

2. Write the ⟍VC‚CV⟍ words with these pronunciations.

   a. /pėr′ mit/   **b.** /fėr′ nish/   **c.** /pėr′ sən/

   d. /sėr′ vəs/   **e.** /fėr′ təl/   **f.** /sėr′ fəs/

3. Write the one-syllable words and the compounds.

4. Write these words from the list.

   a. the snurk   **b.** the snurk's homonym

   c. the synonym of **follow**

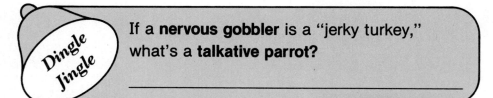 *Working with the Words*

1. Write the **ed** and **ing** forms of the verb /pər mit′/.
Write the plural form of the noun /pėr′ mit/.

2. Write the sentences with correct spellings. Mark the sentences *true* or *false*.

   a. /fėr′ ŦHər môr′/ is an /ad′ vėrb/.

   b. The abbreviation for /kėr′ nəl/ is **Col.**

Dingle Jingle

If a **nervous gobbler** is a "jerky turkey," what's a **talkative parrot?**

Spelling Helps Language

Dictionary Skills

A lexicographer shows the past tense of verbs when **ed** cannot be added.

hurt /hėrt/ *v.* **1.** Cause pain to. **2.** Suffer pain: *My leg hurts.* **hurt, hurting.**

1. Write a dictionary entry for **burst.** Show the past tense form of the entry word.

_____

_____

_____

2. Use spelling words to fill the spaces. Write the sentences with correct spelling, punctuation, and capital letters.

a. Their was an ___ of applause as the runner clear the ___ .

_____

_____

b. does a ___ rank above a major in the army.

_____

_____

c. only one ___ wore a ___ .

_____

Write five questions you would ask the **Sturdy Hurdlers** on page 125 if you were interviewing them for your school paper.

Sound out the /ėr/ words. Then write the rhymes.

skirmish	hurtle	stirrup	percent	curly	third
verdict	curfew	birdhouse	server	servant	jerky
term	whirlpool	shirk	burnt	curdle	hurl

A **bad bird spelling** is a "snurky turkey." Here are some more Dingle Jingles for you to try.

1. A *number one explosion* is a _____ .

2. A *strong little robin* is a _____ .

3. A *magazine for an army officer* is a _____ .

4. A *nervous Thanksgiving fowl* is a _____ .

5. A *solid microbe* must be a _____ .

6. A *female bushytail* must be a _____ .

7. A *strict plant* is a _____ .

8. A *tree bird seat* is a _____ .

9. A *pocketbook stanza* must be a _____ .

10. *Gertrude's pleated garments* are _____ .

11. A *fish bait wriggle* is a _____ .

12. *Preaching in Berlin* is a _____ .

13. A *temple hunt* must be a _____ .

14. A *particular window hanging* is a _____ .

Test

29 Cheer Career Syllables

mere
shear **H**
▽ pierce
fair **H**
fare **H**

dreary
yearly
dairy
prairie

warfare
earache
fearful
cheerleader
chairperson

sincere

declare
despair

aware
revere
career

We hear /ir/ or /ãr/ in every word in the **Cheer Career** list.

We spell /ir/ with *ear*, *eer*, and *ere*.

We spell /ãr/ with *air* and *are*.

 1. Write the nine /ãr/ words. Circle the homonyms.

_____

_____

_____

mere

shear

pierce

fair

fare

drear·y

year·ly

dair·y

prair·ie

war·fare

ear·ache

fear·ful

cheer·lead·er

chair·per·son

sin·cere

de·clare

de·spair

a·ware

re·vere

ca·reer

2. Write the words in which **eer** spells /ir/.

_____

3. Write the /ir/ words that do not have **eer**. Circle the **ere** words.

_____

_____

_____

Working with the Words

1. Write the three-syllable compounds. Underline each syllable with a primary accent.

_____

2. Write the words with these meanings.

a. say **b.** just and honest **c.** go through

_____

3. Write the words with these pronunciations.

a. /sin sir′/ **b.** /prãr′ ē/ **c.** /kə rir′/

_____

4. Complete the sentences using spelling words.

a. The synonym of **honor** is _____ .

b. The homonym of **fare** is _____ .

c. The synonym of **annual** is _____ .

Dingle Jingle

If **infrequent gloom** is "rare despair," what's a **haunted book-lending station**?

_____

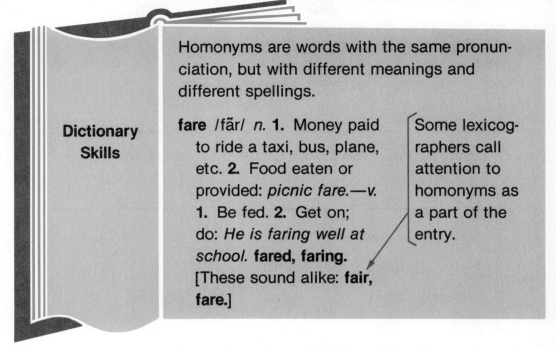

Dictionary Skills

Homonyms are words with the same pronunciation, but with different meanings and different spellings.

fare /fãr/ *n.* **1.** Money paid to ride a taxi, bus, plane, etc. **2.** Food eaten or provided: *picnic fare.—v.* **1.** Be fed. **2.** Get on; do: *He is faring well at school.* **fared, faring.** [These sound alike: **fair, fare.**]

Some lexicographers call attention to homonyms as a part of the entry.

1. Write a dictionary entry for the word **shear,** noting its homonym, **sheer.**

_____

_____

_____

2. Write several sentences about tired pioneers moving westward, almost despairing of finding a homeland. Use **weary, dreary, prairie,** and any other words from this unit that you can.

_____

_____

_____

For your school paper, write an ad for cheerleaders, listing some of the requirements for the position.

Sound out the /ir/ and /ãr/ words.

stare	spare	airy	affair	steer	downstairs
veer	careless	glare	wary	bare	pioneer
spear	veneer	carfare	beware	hardware	repair

In each row, choose the **B** word that goes with the **A** words.

	A			B	
1. oriole	turkey	stork	tern	mare
2. harp	horn	cornet	chorus	organ
3. turbans	shirts	shorts	dairies	scarves
4. clerk	sheriff	nurse	hermit	carpenter
5. horse	deer	squirrel	shark	hare
6. scorpion	serpent	tortoise	horn	turtle
7. star	triangle	circle	square	circus
8. peer	glare	observe	hear	stare
9. steer	veer	turn	share	swerve
10. Virginia	New Jersey	Florida	Oregon	Germany
11. despair	fear	horror	glory	torment
12. Fairbanks	Portland	Hartford	Toronto	Orlando

Test

30 Inhale-Exhale Words

reduce
reflect
require
◊ remove

engage
enable
enlarge
import
impress
inflict
inhale

export
exhale
explode

condense
construct
conduct
compose
combat
compete

Prefixes are word parts we add to words or word roots in order to change the root meaning.

*The **Inhale-Exhale** words have these prefixes:*

re	con, com	in, im, en	ex

1. The **re** prefix means "back" or "again." Write the **re** words. Underline the **re** word that means "shine back."

reduce

reflect

require

remove

engage

enable

enlarge

import

impress

inflict

inhale

export

exhale

explode

condense

construct

conduct

compose

combat

compete

2. The **ex** prefix means "out." Write the **ex** words. Circle the word that means "breathe out."

_____

3. The **en, im,** and **in** prefixes mean "make" or "in." Write the **en, im,** and **in** words. Circle the word that means "make larger."

_____

_____

4. The **con** and **com** prefixes mean "with." Write the **con** and **com** words. Underline the word that means "fight with."

_____

_____

Working with the Words

1. Write the words with these pronunciations. Beside each word, write its root.

  a. /en lärj′/ _____

  b. /im pres′/ _____

  c. /en ā′ bəl/ _____

2. **Port** is a Latin root that means "carry." Write the picture words with the **port** root. Beside each word, write a two-word definition.

  a. _____

  b. _____

134

3. Write one sentence using the verb pronounced /im pôrt′/ and another using the noun pronounced /im′ pôrt/.

_____

_____

_____

4. Endings like **s, ed,** and **ing** are called **inflectional endings.** Write each word below with the **ing** inflectional ending.

a. engage   **b.** remove   **c.** impress

_____

d. exhale   **e.** explode   **f.** reduce

_____

5. Write the picture words. Underline the prefix in each word you write.

a.   **b.**   **c.**

_____

d.   **e.**   **f.**

_____

Dingle Jingle

If to **hire the prophet** is to "engage the sage," what do you do when you **ask for the exam?**

_____

135

Spelling Helps Language

Dictionary Skills

A lexicographer shows prefixes like **en** and **re** as entry words in a dictionary.

en—*prefix.* **1.** Make: *Enable* means *make able.*
2. In: *Enclose* means *close in.*

re—*prefix.* **1.** Again: *Reopen* means *open again.*
2. Back: *Repay* means *pay back.*

1. Write dictionary entries for the prefixes **ex** and **in**. Compare your work with the entries that you find in the Spelling Dictionary.

_____

_____

_____

_____

2. Add the **re** prefix to each word in the box. Write the new words for these meanings.

gain	place	sound	turn	view	read

a. go back   **b.** echo   **c.** study again

_____

d. read again   **e.** get back   **f.** put back

_____

Look again at the picture on page 133. Write five questions a good interviewer would ask the scuba diver.

Sound out these prefix words. Then read the poem aloud.

recruit	condemn	commit	excite	engrave	inquire
request	conclude	command	extract	index	imprison
revolve	conserve	compute	enable	invade	impulse

Hear now the tale of Phineas Phleaphlix,
The man who invented the use of the prefix!
With a wife and ten children and cats to support
Poor Phineas's income quite often fell short.
"The reason," he said, "that I cannot earn more
Is the low price of books that I sell in my store.
If I could sell FAT books, the prices would soar.
Instead of a dollar, I'd charge three or four."
He glared at a thin book, a small dictionary.
"The problem," he said, "is vo′-cab-u-lar-y.
If words would have spare parts, like bits in a drill,
Just think how these pages with entries would fill."
So he invented new words like **repress** and **complain**,
Conclude and **implore**, **inflate** and **explain**,
Enclose and **respect**, **combine** and **concede**,
Import and **inhale**, **enclose** and **exceed**,
Engage and **invite**, **impress** and **confine**,
Compose and **report**, **compare** and **repine**.
Thanks to **re**, **com**, and **con**, **ex**, **im**, **en**, and **in**,
Our Phineas no longer sells books that are thin.
For the words grew by leaps and the pages by bounds,
And his cash register rings now with loud clinking sounds.

Test

illness
weakness
selfishness

argument
employment
agreement
movement

objection
location
correction
pollution

annoyance
ignorance
appearance

absence
evidence
residence

collision
occasion
pension

31 Balance Movement Words

A suffix is a word part added to the end of a word to change its part of speech.

The Balance Movement words have these suffixes:

ness	ment	tion
sion	ance	ence

1. Write the nouns with the **ness** suffix. Then write the adjectives to which the suffix was added.

2. Write the nouns with the **ment** suffix. Then write the verbs from which the nouns were formed.

_____

_____

3. Write **object, locate, correct,** and **pollute.** Then write the nouns that are formed by adding **tion.**

_____

_____

4. Write the nouns with the **ance** and **ence** suffixes.

_____

_____

5. Write the nouns with the **sion** suffix. Underline the word that is formed from the verb **collide.**

_____

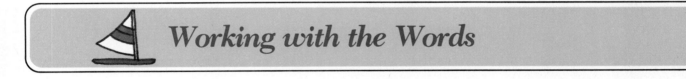

Working with the Words

1. Use spelling words to complete these sentences.

   a. The synonym of **bother** is _____.

   b. The antonym of **presence** is _____.

   c. The synonym of **quarrel** is _____.

   d. The antonym of **strength** is _____.

   e. The synonym of **place** is _____.

   f. The antonym of **health** is _____.

2. Use spelling words to fill the spaces.

   a. **s** spells /zh/ in **collision** and _____.

   b. **s** spells /z/ in _____.

   c. **ear** spells /ir/ in _____.

illness
weakness
selfishness
argument
employment
agreement
movement
objection
location
correction
pollution
annoyance
ignorance
appearance
absence
evidence
residence
collision
occasion
pension

Spelling Helps Language

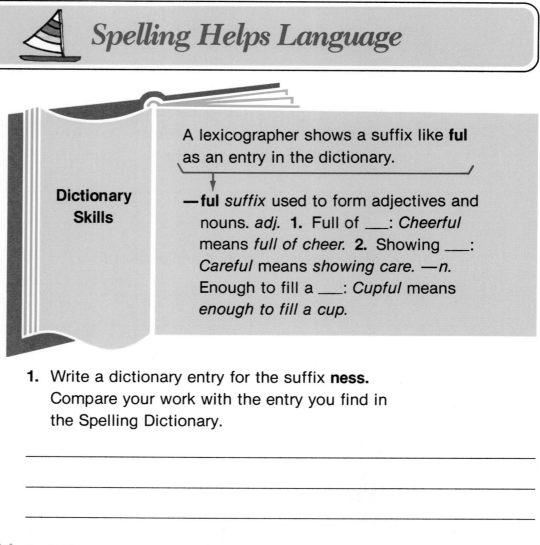

Dictionary Skills

A lexicographer shows a suffix like **ful** as an entry in the dictionary.

—ful *suffix* used to form adjectives and nouns. *adj.* **1.** Full of ___: *Cheerful* means *full of cheer.* **2.** Showing ___: *Careful* means *showing care.* *—n.* Enough to fill a ___: *Cupful* means *enough to fill a cup.*

1. Write a dictionary entry for the suffix **ness**. Compare your work with the entry you find in the Spelling Dictionary.

_____

_____

_____

2. Write the sentences below with correct spelling and correct punctuation.

   a. Your /ə pir′ əns/ is what /ə pirz′/ to those who meat you.

_____

_____

   b. A /kə lizh′ ən/ occurs when to objects /kə līd′/

_____

The four athletes in the picture on page 138 are wind-surfing. Write your own story about their race.

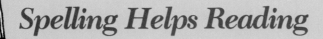

Sound out the suffix words. Then read the story.

wickedness	collection	division	weariness	mission
brightness	settlement	sentence	statement	junction
vacation	ambulance	shipment	inspection	amendment

On many occasions three business men, Mr. Harkness, Mr. Torrence, and Mr. Clarence, had arguments about who had the fastest horse. One horse was named Prudence, one Sensation, and one Sundance. The owners got into action and came to an agreement about the time and location of a race. After the race, the following statements were made.

"Too bad Sundance broke an ankle before the race."

"My brown mare is a fine animal," said Mr. Harkness.

"I call attention to the fact that Prudence has won many racing prizes before this race."

"My horse gave a great performance and, in my judgment, lost because of a recent illness," said Mr. Torrence.

"In all fairness, the black horse won and deserved to win."

"My goodness! Did I fail to mention that this is the first time my horse ever ran in a race?" said Mr. Clarence.

Who owned the winning horse? Which horse won?

Dingle Jingle

If a **story dispute** is "fiction friction," what is **adding halves and thirds?**

_____

Test

preserve
pretend
prefer
prescribe
preview

proceed
proclaim
propose
promote

unable
unequal
unusual

decline
despise
decrease
descend

disgust
dismiss
discard
discharge

Prefixes change the meanings of the word roots to which they are added.

These prefixes are used in the Unusual Descent list:

pre	pro	un
de	dis	

1. The **pre** prefix means "before." Write the **pre** words. Circle the word that means "like better than, or before, others."

2. The **pro** prefix means "forward." Write the **pro** words. Underline the word that means "move forward."

_____

3. The **de** prefix means "down" or "from." Write the **de** words. Underline the word that means "go down."

_____

4. The **dis** prefix means "down" or "opposite of." Write the **dis** words. Underline the word that means "throw away; give up as useless."

_____

5. The **un** prefix means "not." Write the words that mean "not able," "not equal," and "not usual."

_____

Working with the Words

1. Write the words with these sounds and spellings.

   a. sc spells /s/   **b. ge** spells /j/   **c. ss** spells /s/

   _____

   d. ai spells /ā/   **e. ea** spells /ē/   **f. ee** spells /ē/

   _____

2. Write the **ed** forms of these words.

   a. discard   **b.** discharge   **c.** propose

   _____

Dingle Jingle

If **get rid of the sentry** is "discard the guard," what's **fire the sergeant**?

_____

preserve
pretend
prefer
prescribe
preview
proceed
proclaim
propose
promote
unable
unequal
unusual
decline
despise
decrease
descend
disgust
dismiss
discard
discharge

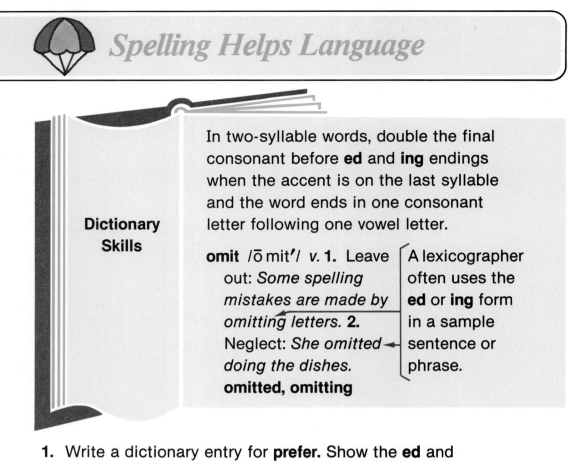

Spelling Helps Language

Dictionary Skills

In two-syllable words, double the final consonant before **ed** and **ing** endings when the accent is on the last syllable and the word ends in one consonant letter following one vowel letter.

omit /ō mit′/ *v.* **1.** Leave out: *Some spelling mistakes are made by omitting letters.* **2.** Neglect: *She omitted doing the dishes.* **omitted, omitting**

A lexicographer often uses the **ed** or **ing** form in a sample sentence or phrase.

1. Write a dictionary entry for **prefer.** Show the **ed** and **ing** forms of the entry word and use the **ed** form in a sentence or phrase.

_____

_____

_____

2. Write a short paragraph about a person who despises tennis and prefers baseball. Tell what happens when this person pretends to like tennis to impress a friend.

_____

_____

_____

_____

Write a dictionary definition of the word **trampoline** and tell where we got the word.

Sound out the prefix words. Read the story.

presume	produce	unfinished	precede	delay	dispose
untrue	uneasy	dissolve	progress	discount	undo
predict	debate	unknown	prevent	displace	prepare

An elderly king, realizing that his health was declining, decided to choose one of his two children to succeed him on the throne. Unhappily, the children, a son and a daughter, preferred to devote their time to racing horses and did not pretend to prepare themselves to rule the country.

The provoked father at last became so disgusted that he proceeded to proclaim a most unusual decree.

"To prevent discord and preserve peace, we will have a horse race to determine who shall become ruler," he announced. "The winner will be the one whose horse loses the race."

Each child presumed the other would unfairly slow his horse down. Deeply distressed, they protested bitterly.

"Very well," said the king. "We can depend on our wise Ben Ali to propose a way to prevent cheating. Ali will not disappoint me, for his wisdom is profound."

And indeed, Ali did dispose of the problem. He gave both children a command in two words that made sure the race would be fair. Can you guess the two words?

How many **un** words? _____ **pro** words? _____

de words? _____ **dis** words? _____ **pre** words? _____

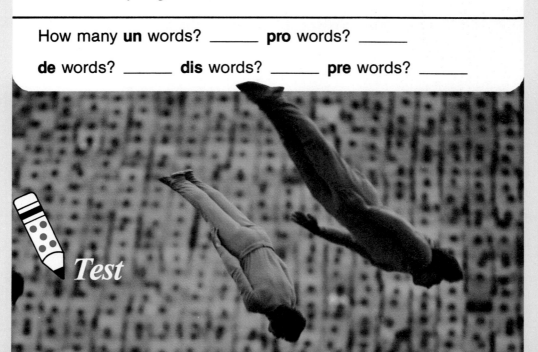

Test

successful
powerful
graceful

faul**t**less
hee**d**less
mat**ch**less

hum**or**ous
hazar**d**ous
mountain**ous**
treacher**ous**

assist**ant**
atten**d**ant
ignor**ant**

opp**on**ent
contin**ent**
promin**ent**

suit**able**
reason**able**

aud**ible**
vis**ible**

The Graceful Opponent list has these suffixes:

ful	less	ous	ant

ent	able	ible

1. Write the adjectives with the **ful** and **less** suffixes.
Underline the word that means "careless."

2. Write the words with **ant** and **ent** suffixes. Underline the four words used as nouns.

_____

_____

3. Write the adjectives with **able** and **ible** suffixes. Circle the antonym of **invisible.**

_____

4. Write the adjectives with the **ous** suffix. Circle the snurk and its synonym.

_____

Working with the Words

1. Write adjectives from the list to describe the pictures.

a.   b.   c.

_____

2. Write spelling words to complete these sentences.

a. The synonym of **fitting** is _____ .

b. The antonym of **unsuitable** is _____ .

c. The synonym of **helper** is _____ .

Dingle Jingle

If a **wise scholar** is a "prudent student," what's an **agreeable game bird?**

_____

successful
powerful
graceful
faultless
heedless
matchless
humorous
hazardous
mountainous
treacherous
assistant
attendant
ignorant
opponent
continent
prominent
suitable
reasonable
audible
visible

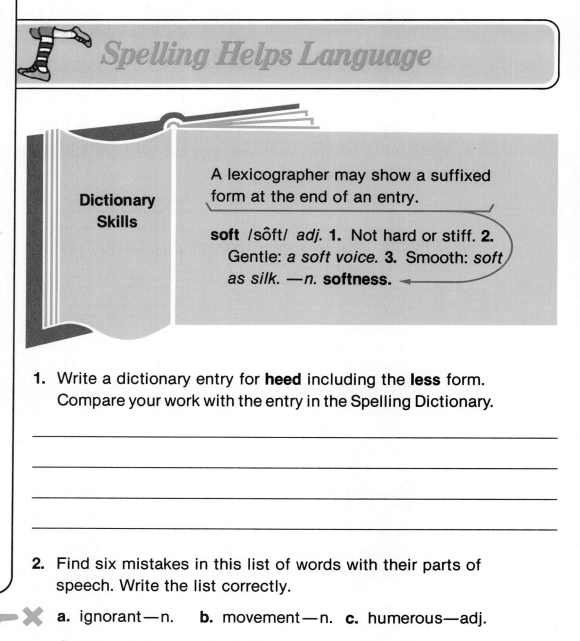

Spelling Helps Language

Dictionary Skills

A lexicographer may show a suffixed form at the end of an entry.

soft /sôft/ *adj.* **1.** Not hard or stiff. **2.** Gentle: *a soft voice.* **3.** Smooth: *soft as silk.* —*n.* **softness.**

1. Write a dictionary entry for **heed** including the **less** form. Compare your work with the entry in the Spelling Dictionary.

_____

_____

_____

_____

2. Find six mistakes in this list of words with their parts of speech. Write the list correctly.

a. ignorant—n.   **b.** movement—n.   **c.** humorous—adj.

d. occassion—n.   **e.** heedless—n.   **f.** pension—n.

g. successful—n.   **h.** arguement—n.   **i.** despise—v.

_____

_____

Look again at the picture on page 146. Choose one of the **Graceful Opponent** starters as the winner and write a newspaper report on the race results.

Sound out the suffix words. Then read the story.

visible	fruitful	evident	helpful	accident	sensible
forcible	lawful	fragrant	endless	abundant	homeless
president	vigorous	usable	gallant	honorable	generous

Once upon a time a powerful and successful ruler had to make a hazardous trip over dangerous mountainous land.

"It is quite possible that I may never return," he said. "It would evidently be sensible to appoint a suitable assistant to rule while I am absent."

Wishing to find the most intelligent person on the entire continent, the king proposed the following puzzle:

If you have only one match in a room where
there are an oil lamp, a wood-burning oven,
and a fireplace, which should you light first?

"The person with the best answer is to be rewarded with this honorable post," he stated.

Numerous capable and prominent thinkers and diligent scholars constantly turned up with different answers. At last a humble kitchen attendant in the king's palace came up with the most reasonable answer of all. What was it?

able/ible words? _____   **ant/ent** words? _____

Test

34 Resistance Excitement Words

discussion
resistance
procession
instruction
uneasiness
impeachment
disturbance
commotion
enlargement
prescription
conversation
prevention
confusion
independence
introduction
immigrant
unselfishness
depression
existence
improvement

In each **Resistance Excitement** *word…*

spell the prefix,

spell the root,

spell the suffix.

1. Write the words with the **im, in,** and **intro** prefixes. Underline the word that means "teaching."

2. Write the words with the **con** and **com** prefixes. Underline the two nouns with nearly the same meaning.

_____

3. Write the words with the **de** and **dis** prefixes. Underline the word that means "a low place."

_____

4. Write the words with the **pre** and **pro** prefixes. Underline the word that means "persons marching forward."

_____

5. Write the words with the **un, ex, re,** and **en** prefixes.

_____

_____

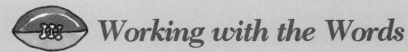 ## Working with the Words

1. Write the **ment** words in alphabetical order.

_____

2. Write the spelling words that complete the sentences.

  a. The word pronounced /dis tėr′ bəns/ is _____ .

  b. The word pronounced /rē zis′ təns/ is _____ .

  c. The noun form of **instruct** is _____ .

  d. The noun form of **prescribe** is _____ .

  e. The word pronounced /kən fū′ zhən/ is _____ .

  f. The noun form of **discuss** is _____ .

Dingle Jingle

If a **Chinese raid** is an "Asian invasion," what's a **talk with the Soviets?**

_____

discussion
resistance
procession
instruction
uneasiness
impeachment
disturbance
commotion
enlargement
prescription
conversation
prevention
confusion
independence
introduction
immigrant
unselfishness
depression
existence
improvement

3. Write the nouns formed from these adjectives.

    a. uneasy   **b.** unselfish   **c.** independent

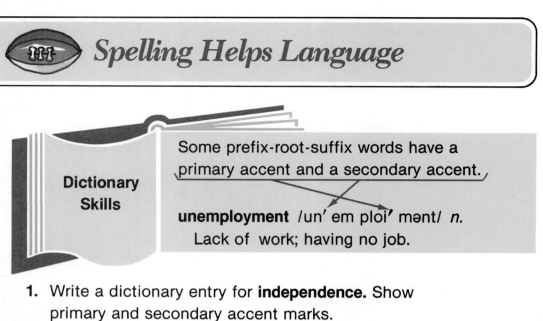

Spelling Helps Language

Dictionary Skills

Some prefix-root-suffix words have a primary accent and a secondary accent.

unemployment /un′ em ploi′ mənt/ *n.*
Lack of work; having no job.

1. Write a dictionary entry for **independence.** Show primary and secondary accent marks.

_____

_____

_____

2. Join the prefixes, roots, and suffixes to write six new prefix-root-suffix words.

Prefix		Root		Suffix	
un	de	pan	cep	ness	ence
con	ex	fair	appoint	tion	ment
com	dis	fes	pend	sion	ion

_____

_____

Look again at the **Resistance Excitement** picture on page 150. Write what you would say if you were telecasting the action.

Sound out the words. Then read the story.

commandment	extension	department	projection
exception	reduction	invasion	enrollment
promotion	unevenness	excitement	explosion
enrichment	unhappiness	compartment	disappointment

When the intelligent attendant was chosen to rule during the king's absence, there was great uneasiness among the nobles. Indeed, they made quite a commotion, and there was even some sly conversation about impeachment.

When the king returned safely from his expedition, however, he found that all government departments, without exception, were in fine condition. When the king made the announcement that his daughter, the lovely princess, was to wed, the confident young attendant joined a long procession of suitors for her hand. Again the nobles demanded that the competition be limited to those of royal blood.

Excitement grew at the king's decision to issue a proclamation that an examination would be given to determine the winner. The king's examination was as follows:

A merchant left his three children seven barrels full of wine, seven barrels half full of wine, and seven empty barrels. Each child was to have the same number of full, half-full, and empty barrels. How can this be done?

The attendant had a clever explanation. Do you?

 *Test*

reluctant
disagreeable
previous
responsible
excellent
unlawful
contagious
regardless
dependent
untruthful
unpleasant
impossible
enjoyable
industrious
innocent
comfortable
dependable
invisible
confident
unskillful

In each Reluctant Receiver word...

spell the prefix,

spell the root,

spell the suffix.

1. Write the **able** and **ible** words. Underline the suffix in each word you write.

_____

_____

_____

2. Write the **ful** and **less** words. Underline the suffixes.

_____

3. Write the **ant** and **ent** words. Underline the suffixes.

_____

_____

4. Write the **ous** words.

_____

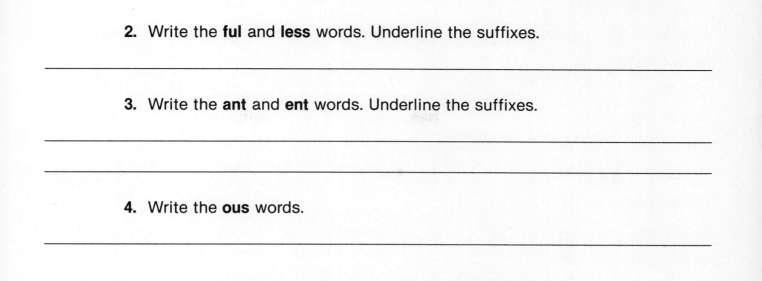

Working with the Words

1. Write the adjectives that are formed from these verbs.

    a. disagree   **b.** respond   **c.** regard

_____

    d. excel   **e.** enjoy   **f.** confide

_____

2. Write the <u>misspelled</u> words correctly.

    a. truthful   agreable   _____

    b. visable   uncomfortable   _____

    c. possible   uncertian   _____

    d. independant   dependable   _____

    e. contageous   regardless   _____

    f. previous   reluctent   _____

Write a short paragraph telling why the "receiver" in the photograph on page 154 is so "reluctant."

reluctant
disagreeable
previous
responsible
excellent
unlawful
contagious
regardless
dependent
untruthful
unpleasant
impossible
enjoyable
industrious
innocent
comfortable
dependable
invisible
confident
unskillful

Spelling Helps Language

Dictionary Skills

A lexicographer shows many prefixed words as separate dictionary entries.

inconvenient /in′ kən vēn′ yənt/ *adj.* Not convenient; troublesome; causing bother, difficulty, or discomfort: *It is inconvenient for you to leave now.*

1. Write a dictionary entry for **invisible.** Compare your work with the entry in the Spelling Dictionary.

_____

_____

_____

2. Join the prefixes, roots, and suffixes to spell new prefix-root-suffix adjectives. Use each printed word part in the boxes.

Prefix		Root		Suffix	
im	un	mark	port	ful	able
im	con	vent	prob	ent	able
pre	re	help	veni	ant	able

_____

_____

Dingle Jingle

If being both **dependable and agreeable** is being "reliable and pliable," what's being both **stubborn and clumsy?**

_____

156

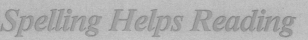
Sound out the prefix-root-suffix words.

delightful	improbable	remorseless	incredible
regretful	reliable	convenient	disgraceful
indifferent	consistent	independent	unimportant

For each sentence, find the matching statement below.

1. Disagreeable deportment is frequently responsible for unpleasant disturbances. _____

2. Reliable construction is always dependent upon competent craftsmen. _____

3. Excellent references are rarely reliable without previous employment experience. _____

4. Insufficient information is not infrequently the cause of incredible recommendations. _____

5. Industrious instructors have little inclination to engage in unimportant discussions. _____

A. If you want good buildings, you need good workers.

B. Busy teachers don't like to waste time talking.

C. Bad suggestions are often made because people don't have enough facts.

D. Bad behavior causes noise.

E. It's hard to believe good reports about a person if he or she hasn't worked before.

 *Test*

36 Elevator Operator Words

ordinary
ability
activity
majority
accompany

radiator
elevator
operator
caterpillar
altogether

material
colonial
mechanical

appreciate
circumference
certificate
affectionate
agriculture
patriotic
automatic

The words in the **Elevator Operator** list are four-syllable words, some with soft-syllable endings.

Divide the long words into eye-syllables to make them easier to spell.

1. Write the eye-syllables of these words.

   a. appreciate _____ _____ _____ _____

   b. agriculture _____ _____ _____ _____

2. Write the eye-syllables of these words.

   a. affectionate   _____   _____   _____   _____

   b. circumference   _____   _____   _____   _____

   c. patriotic   _____   _____   _____   _____

   d. certificate   _____   _____   _____   _____

3. Write the words that end in /əl/ or /ər/.

   _____

   _____

4. Write the words that have the soft-syllable /ē/ ending. Underline the word that means "more than half."

   _____

   _____

5. Write the words with these sounds and spellings.

   a. ch = /k/   **b. th** = /ŦH/   **c. au** = /ô/

   _____

Working with the Words

1. **Proofread** the list of four-syllable words. Write the <u>misspelled</u> words correctly.

   a. altogether   abillity   _____

   b. circumferance   certificate   _____

   c. automatic   affectionat   _____

   d. agriculture   appreshiate   _____

   e. coloniel   radiator   _____

   f. elevator   caterpiller   _____

   g. acompany   ordinary   _____

or din ar y
a bil i ty
ac tiv i ty
ma jor i ty
ac com pan y
ra di a tor
el e va tor
op er a tor
cat er pil lar
al to geth er
ma ter i al
co lon i al
me chan i cal
ap pre ci ate
cir cum fer ence
cer tif i cate
af fec tion ate
ag ri cul ture
pa tri o tic
au to mat ic

2. Use words from the spelling list to complete the sentences below.

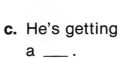

a. That ___ is sick.

b. The ___ is crowded.

c. He's getting a ___ .

d. She seems very ___ .

e. The boy is quite ___ .

f. That's a hot ___ .

3. Complete the chart.

a. patriot *(n.)* _____ *(adj.)*

b. _____ *(n.)* affectionate *(adj).*

c. appreciate *(v.)* _____ *(n.)*

d. _____ *(v.)* operator *(n.)*

e. mechanical *(adj.)* _____ *(n.)*

f. _____ *(n.)* active *(adj.)*

g. accompaniment *(n.)* _____ *(v.)*

h. _____ *(n.)* agricultural *(adj.)*

Dingle Jingle

If a **reptile lift** is an "alligator elevator," what's a **camel's word book**?

_____

Spelling Helps Language

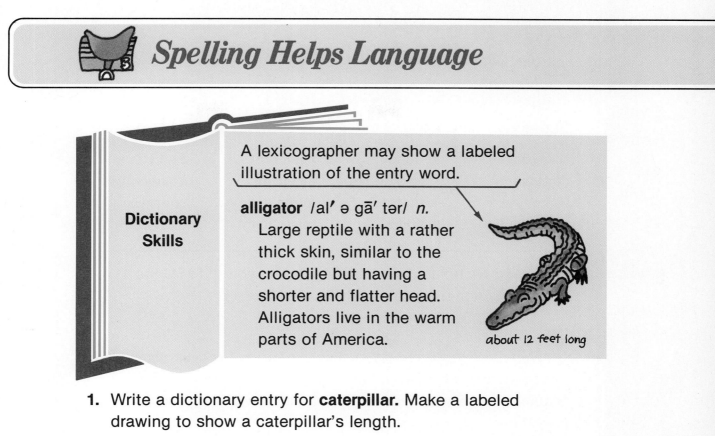

Dictionary Skills

A lexicographer may show a labeled illustration of the entry word.

alligator /al′ ə gā′ tər/ *n.* Large reptile with a rather thick skin, similar to the crocodile but having a shorter and flatter head. Alligators live in the warm parts of America.

about 12 feet long

1. Write a dictionary entry for **caterpillar.** Make a labeled drawing to show a caterpillar's length.

2. Write the word in each row that would be an entry word in a regular dictionary.

   a. alligators   ability   majorities   _____

   b. caterpillar   appreciated   operating   _____

3. Write a sentence about children with unusual skill in working with machinery. Use three of these words: **ability, mechanical, majority,** and **altogether.**

Write your own story about Pegasus, the winged horse. Use an encyclopedia.

161

Sound out the words.

territory	epidemic	cemetery	literature
dictionary	temperature	scientific	democratic
rectangular	escalator	sympathetic	energetic
ambassador	electrical	customary	irregular

Proofread Nicholas Knitpicker's letter as you did in Units 11, 17, and 24. Again, write a reply to Nicholas.

Dear Editor:

   Well, here you have my customary letter. I congratulate you for a superior publication. I found only one error in your arithmetic quiz, and I am confident that you will appreciate my calling it to your attention.

   The quiz included a question which asked what a person's body temperature would read on a Celsius thermometer if the Fahrenheit reading showed normal body temperature. The answer given was 35 degrees. As normal body temperature is 98.6 degrees on a Fahrenheit thermometer, the Celsius reading would be 37 degrees. Please investigate immediately.

   The scientific material was excellent, and your geography quiz had no errors. I trust that you will lend a sympathetic ear to my appeal to be appointed to your staff. I optimistically await a favorable reply.

Affectionately yours,

Nicholas Knitpicker

How many mistakes did you find in the letter?

S _____ P _____ C _____ E _____ F _____

Test

SPELLING DICTIONARY

Aa

ability /ə bil′ ə tē/ *n.* **1.** Power: *the ability to work.* **2.** Skill: *She has great ability as an actress.* **3.** Talent: *musical ability. pl.* **abilities.**

absence /ab′ səns/ *n.* **1.** Being away: *absence from school.* **2.** Time of being away.

absorb /əb zôrb′/ *v.* **1.** Take in; suck up: *The sponge absorbed all the water.* **2.** Interest very much: *The boy was so absorbed by the baseball game that he did not notice the rain.*

absorbing /əb zôrb′ ing/ *adj.* Extremely interesting: *The explorer told an absorbing story.*

accompany /ə kum′ pə nē/ *v.* **1.** Go along with: *May I accompany you on your walk?* **2.** Be or happen along with: *rain accompanied by strong wind.* **accompanied, accompanying.**

account /ə kount′/ *n.* **1.** Explanation. **2.** Statement of money received and spent. —*v.* Consider; hold to be true: *Solomon was accounted wise.*

acorn /ā′ kôrn/ *n.* The nut of an oak tree.

activity /ak tiv′ ə tē/ *n.* **1.** Being active: *Children engage in more physical activity than old people.* **2.** Action: *the activities of the enemy.* **3.** Thing to do: *My favorite activity is playing football. pl.* **activities.**

actor /ak′ tər/ *n.* Person who acts on the stage, in movies, on television, or over radio.

adopt /ə dopt′/ *v.* Take for one's own: *We adopted the stray kitten.*

adult /ə dult′/ *or* /ad′ ult/ *adj.* Full-grown. —*n.* **1.** Grown-up person. **2.** Plant or animal grown to full size or strength.

affectionate /ə fek′ shən ət/ *adj.* Loving; fond: *an affectionate puppy.*

agent /ā′ jənt/ *n.* **1.** Person or company that acts for another. **2.** Any power or cause that produces an effect: *Yeast is an important agent in causing bread to rise.*

agreement /ə grē′ mənt/ *n.* **1.** An understanding; a contract or treaty. **2.** Harmony: *There was perfect agreement between the two friends.*

agriculture /ag′ rə kul′ chər/ *n.* Farming; the raising of crops and farm animals.

airline /ār′ līn′/ *n.* System of transportation of people and things by aircraft.

allow /ə lou′/ *v.* Let; permit.

alloy /al′ oi/ *n.* **1.** Metal made by melting and mixing two or more metals. Brass is an alloy of copper and zinc. **2.** An inferior metal mixed with a more valuable one: *His ring is not pure gold; there is some alloy in it.*

alter /ôl′ tər/ *v.* **1.** Change; make different: *The suit was too large until the tailor altered it.* **2.** Become different: *Since her vacation, her outlook has altered.*

altogether /ôl′ tə geҭH′ ər/ *adv.* Completely; entirely: *The house was altogether destroyed.*

annoy /ə noi′/ *v.* Make somewhat angry; disturb: *The baby annoys his sister.*

annoyance /ə noi′ əns/ *n.* **1.** Feeling of dislike or trouble: *She showed annoyance at the delay.* **2.** Something that causes a feeling of dislike or trouble; disturbance: *Heavy traffic on our street is an annoyance.*

anthem /an′ thəm/ *n.* Song of praise or patriotism.

apart /ə pärt′/ *adv.* **1.** In pieces; in separate parts: *She took the motor apart.* **2.** Away from each other: *They stood apart.* **3.** To one side; aside: *She set some money apart for a new coat.*

/a/ ran /ā/ rain /ā/ care /ä/ car /e/ hen /ē/ he /ėr/ her /i/ in /ī/ ice /o/ not /ō/ no /ô/ off /u/ us /ū/ use /ü/ tool /u̇/ took /ou/ cow /oi/ boy /ch/ church /hw/ when /ng/ sing /sh/ ship /ҭH/ this /th/ thin /zh/ vision /ə/ about, taken, pencil, lemon, circus

appeal /ə pēl′/ v. **1.** Make an earnest request; ask for help. **2.** Be attractive, interesting, or enjoyable: *Football appeals to me more than baseball.* —n. **1.** An earnest request; a call for help. **2.** Attraction; interest.

appearance /ə pir′ əns/ n. **1.** A coming into sight: *the appearance of a comet.* **2.** Coming before the public: *the actor's first appearance.* **3.** Outward look: *the appearance of the old house.*

applaud /ə plôd′/ v. **1.** Express approval by clapping hands, shouting, etc. **2.** Approve; praise.

appoint /ə point′/ v. **1.** Name a person for a position or job; choose. **2.** Decide on; set.

appreciate /ə prē′ shē āt′/ v. **1.** Value; recognize the worth of: *He appreciates music.* **2.** Be thankful for: *I appreciate your help.* **appreciated, appreciating.**

approach /ə prōch′/ v. Come near or nearer. —n. **1.** The way by which a person or thing is reached: *The approach to the house was a narrow driveway.* **2.** Act of coming near or nearer: *the approach of a storm.*

approve /ə prüv′/ v. **1.** Think or speak well of; be pleased with. **2.** Consent to: *Congress approved the bill.* **3.** Give a favorable opinion: *approve of an action.* **approved, approving.**

argument /är′ gū mənt/ n. **1.** Discussion by persons who disagree; dispute. **2.** Reason or reasons given for or against something.

armor /är′ mər/ n. A covering, usually of metal or leather, worn to protect the body in fighting.

arouse /ə rouz′/ v. **1.** Excite; stir into action. **2.** Awaken. **aroused, arousing.**

assault /ə sôlt′/ n. A sudden, vigorous attack. —v. Make an assault on: *The army assaulted the fort.*

assistant /ə sist′ ənt/ n. Helper; aid: *the teacher's assistant.* —adj. Helping: *an assistant nurse.*

assort /ə sôrt′/ v. **1.** Sort out; classify. **2.** Agree in sort or kind; fall into a class.

athlete /ath′ lēt/ n. Person trained in the exercise of physical strength, speed, and skill: *Baseball players are athletes.*

atlas /at′ ləs/ n. Book of maps. Named for *Atlas,* a giant in Greek myths who supported the heavens on his shoulders. A picture of this giant was common on the first page in early collections of maps. *pl.* **atlases.**

atom /at′ əm/ n. Very small particle; tiny bit.

attendant /ə ten′ dənt/ n. Person who waits on another. —adj. Accompanying: *Sneezing is an attendant discomfort of a cold.*

audible /ôd′ ə bəl/ adj. Able to be heard; loud enough to be heard: *Her soft voice was barely audible at the back of the room.*

automatic /ô′ tə mat′ ik/ adj. **1.** Moving or acting by itself: *an automatic elevator.* **2.** Done without thought or attention: *Breathing and swallowing are automatic.*

autumn /ô′ təm/ n. Season of the year between summer and winter; fall.

aware /ə wãr′/ or /ə wer′/ adj. Having knowledge; conscious: *They were aware of the danger.*

awkward /ôk′ wərd/ adj. **1.** Not graceful in movement: *an awkward dancer.* **2.** Not easily handled: *an awkward corner to turn.* **3.** Embarrassing: *an awkward question.* syn. **clumsy; ungraceful.** ant. **graceful.**

Bb

backbone /bak′ bōn′/ n. **1.** The main bone down the middle of the back; spine. **2.** The most important part.

backtrack /bak′ trak′/ v. **1.** Go back over a course or path. **2.** Withdraw from an undertaking, position, etc.

bamboo /bam bü′/ n. Woody, treelike grass with a tall, stiff, hollow stem, used in making canes, fishing poles, furniture, etc. *pl.* **bamboos.**

barbershop /bär′ bər shop′/ n. Shop in which haircuts are given.

barley /bär′ lē/ n. A grasslike plant grown in cool climates and used for its grain.

basin /bā′ sən/ n. **1.** Wide, shallow dish; bowl. **2.** Amount a basin can hold: *a basin of water.* **3.** Shallow area containing water: *Part of the harbor is a basin for yachts.*

baton /bə ton′/ n. The staff or stick used by

the leader of an orchestra or band for beating time to the music.

beehive /bē′ hīv′/ *n.* **1.** Hive, or house, for bees. **2.** Busy, swarming place: *a beehive of activity.*

beeline /bē′ līn′/ *n.* The straightest way or line between two places, such as a bee takes in returning to its hive.

bench /bench/ *n.* **1.** A long seat, usually of wood or stone. **2.** A strong, heavy table used by a carpenter or by any worker with tools. *pl.* **benches.**

beneath /bē nēth′/ *prep.* Below; under: *beneath a tree.* —*adv.* In a lower place: *The nut fell from the tree to a spot beneath.*

between /bē twēn′/ *prep.* **1.** In the time or space separating two objects, points, or places: *There are many cities between Chicago and New York.* **2.** From one to the other of: *There is a new highway between Chicago and St. Louis.* **3.** Having to do with: *There was a fight between the two boys.* **4.** In regard to one or the other: *We must choose between the two books.*

billboard /bil′ bôrd′/ *n.* Outdoor signboard.

bind /bīnd/ *v.* **1.** Tie together; hold together; fasten. **2.** Hold by some force; restrain. **3.** Put a bandage on. **bound, binding.**

blare /blãr/ *v.* Make a loud, harsh sound: *The trumpets blared to announce the king's arrival.* —*n.* Loud, harsh sound: *The blare of the horns was heard across the town.* **blared, blaring.**

blight /blīt/ *n.* **1.** Any disease that causes plants to wither or decay. **2.** Anything that causes destruction or ruin. —*v.* **1.** Cause to wither or decay. **2.** Destroy; ruin.

blister /blis′ tər/ *n.* Small baglike place under the skin filled with watery matter. —*v.* **1.** Raise a blister on. **2.** Attack with sharp words.

blockade /blok′ ād/ *n.* Control of what goes in and out of a place by the use of an army or navy. —*v.* Control what goes in or out of a place by using an army or navy. **blockaded, blockading.**

blond /blond/ *adj.* **1.** Light in color: *blond hair.* **2.** Having yellow or light-brown hair: *Have you seen that blond boy with my sister?* —*n.* Person with blond hair. (Spelled **blonde** when referring to a girl or a woman.)

blowout /blō′ out′/ *n.* The bursting of an automobile tire.

bluegrass /blü′ gras′/ *n.* Grass with bluish-green stems.

boast /bōst/ *v.* **1.** Speak too well of oneself or what one owns. **2.** Be proud of. **3.** Have something to be proud of: *Our school boasts a new library.* —*n.* Statement in praise of oneself.

bonus /bō′ nəs/ *n.* Something extra given in addition to what is due. *pl.* **bonuses.**

bookmark /bůk′ märk′/ *n.* A ribbon or the like placed in a book to mark a certain place.

bookstore /bůk′ stôr′/ *n.* Store where books are sold.

booth /büth/ *n.* **1.** Place where goods are shown or sold at a fair, market, or convention. **2.** Small, closed place for a telephone or motion-picture projector. *pl.* **booths** /büᴛʜz/ *or* /büths/.

borrow /bôr′ ō/ *v.* **1.** Get something from another person with the understanding that it must be returned. **2.** Get and use as your own: *The word "canoe" was borrowed from the Indians.*

bough /bou/ *n.* **1.** One of the main branches of a tree. **2.** Branch cut from a tree.

bound /bound/ *v.* See **bind.** *He was bound with ropes to the tree.*

boycott /boi′ kot/ *v.* Join together against and have nothing to do with a person, business, or nation in order to force an action or to punish. —*n.* The act of boycotting a person, business, or nation.

boyhood /boi′ hůd′/ *n.* **1.** Time during which one is a boy. **2.** Boys: *The boyhood of the nation produces leaders of the future.*

/a/ ran /ā/ rain /ã/ care /ä/ car /e/ hen /ē/ he /ėr/ her /i/ in /ī/ ice /o/ not /ō/ no /ô/ off /u/ us
/ū/ use /ü/ tool /ů/ took /ou/ cow /oi/ boy /ch/ church /hw/ when /ng/ sing /sh/ ship /ᴛʜ/ this
/th/ thin /zh/ vision /ə/ about, taken, pencil, lemon, circus

bray /brā/ *v.* Make a loud, harsh cry like that of a donkey. —*n.* Loud, harsh cry of a donkey; any loud, harsh cry.

brew /brü/ *v.* **1.** Make a drink by soaking, boiling, or mixing. **2.** Plot; plan; bring about: *The boys are brewing some mischief.* **3.** Begin to form: *The storm is brewing.* —*n.* Drink that is brewed.

broil /broil/ *v.* **1.** Cook by putting or holding directly over or under heat or fire. **2.** Be very hot: *You will broil in this hot sun.*

broth /brôth/ *n.* Thin soup: *This broth is made from meat and vegetables.*

brow /brou/ *n.* **1.** Forehead. **2.** Eyebrow. **3.** Top of a slope: *the brow of the hill.*

browbeat /brou′ bēt′/ *v.* Bully; frighten by harsh words or threats.

browse /brouz/ *v.* **1.** Skim through a book reading passages here and there. **2.** Look through a group of things in search of something of interest: *browse through a library.* **browsed, browsing.**

brutal /brü′ təl/ *adj.* Coarse and savage; cruel: *a brutal beating.*

buckle /buk′ əl/ *n.* **1.** Fastening for two loose ends of a belt, strap, etc. **2.** Metal ornament for a shoe. **3.** A distortion; bulge. —*v.* **1.** Fasten together with a buckle. **2.** Bulge; bend; wrinkle. **buckled, buckling.**

budget /buj′ ət/ *n.* A plan of the way money can be spent for various purposes. —*v.* Make a plan for spending or using: *Budget your time carefully.*

bugle /bū′ gəl/ *n.* Musical instrument like a small trumpet, made of brass.

build /bild/ *v.* **1.** Make by putting materials together. **2.** Develop: *A lawyer builds his case on facts.* **built, building.**

bulge /bulj/ *v.* Swell outward: *Our pockets bulged with candy.* **bulged, bulging.** —*n.* An outward swelling.

bulky /bul′ kē/ *adj.* Taking up too much space; large; hard to handle. **bulkier, bulkiest.**

burner /bėr′ nər/ *n.* Thing or part that burns, or works by heat: *Some stoves are gas burners; others are oil burners.*

burst /bėrst/ *v.* **1.** Break open or apart suddenly: *The flowers burst into bloom.* **2.** Ex-plode: *The bomb will burst.* **3.** Go, come, or do suddenly: *The children burst into the room without knocking.* **4.** Be very full: *The barns are bursting with grain.* **burst, bursting.** —*n.* **1.** Outbreak: *a burst of laughter.* **2.** Sudden display: *a burst of speed.*

Cc

cactus /kak′ təs/ *n.* Plant with spines on thick stems but usually without leaves. *pl.* **cactuses** or **cacti** /kak′ tī/.

camel /kam′ əl/ *n.* Large, four-footed animal with one or two humps on its back.

canvas /kan′ vəs/ *n.* **1.** Strong cloth with a coarse weave used to make tents and sails. **2.** Piece of canvas on which oil painting is made. *pl.* **canvases.** —*adj.* Made of canvas: *The canvas sails of the boats were torn in the storms.*

carbon /kär′ bən/ *n.* The substance that coal, charcoal, and graphite are made of.

career /kə rir′/ *n.* Occupation; profession; life's work: *Many men and women choose the Navy as their career.*

carefree /kãr′ frē′/ *adj.* Without worry; happy; gay: *The children spent a carefree summer.*

cargo /kär′ gō/ *n.* Freight carried by a ship or plane: *The ships were carrying cargoes of wheat and rice.* *pl.* **cargoes** or **cargos.**

carton /kärt′ ən/ *n.* Box made of pasteboard.

cartoon /kär tün′/ *n.* **1.** Sketch or drawing that shows persons, things, or events in an exaggerated way: *Political cartoons often represent the United States as a tall man called Uncle Sam.* **2.** Comic strip.

cartridge /kärt′ rij/ *n.* **1.** Case for holding gun powder. **2.** Small container holding a roll of camera film, ink for a pen, etc.

caterpillar /kat′ ər pil′ ər/ *n.* Larva, or worm-like form, in which insects such as the butterfly and the moth hatch. A caterpillar is about 2½ inches long.

cedar /sē′ dər/ *n.* Evergreen tree with branches that spread widely and with fragrant, reddish, durable wood.

cell /sel/ *n.* **1.** Small room in a prison or monastery. **2.** Any small, hollow space: *the cells of a honeycomb.* **3.** A very small unit of living matter.

certificate /sər tif′ ə kət/ *n.* Written or printed statement that may be used as proof of a fact: *a birth certificate.*

chairperson /chãr′ pėr′ sən/ *n.* **1.** Person in charge of a meeting. **2.** Person at the head of a committee.

chapter /chap′ tər/ *n.* Main division of a book, written about a particular part of the subject or story.

chart /chärt/ *n.* **1.** Map. **2.** Sheet of information arranged in pictures, tables, or diagrams. —*v.* Make a map or chart of: *The captain charted the course of the ship.*

cheat /chēt/ *v.* Deceive; trick; play, work or do business in a dishonest way. —*n.* Person who deceives others; fraud.

cheerleader /chir′ lē′ dər/ *n.* Person who leads the cheers for a team playing football, baseball, etc.

chide /chīd/ *v.* Find fault with; blame; scold. **chided, chiding.**

chimney /chim′ nē/ *n.* **1.** An upright structure of brick or stone, connected to a fireplace or furnace, to make a draft and carry away smoke. **2.** Glass tube placed around the flame of a lamp. *pl.* **chimneys.**

choir /kwīr/ *n.* Group of singers; group of singers in a church.

chorus /kôr′ əs/ *n.* **1.** Group of singers such as a choir. **2.** Song sung by many singers together. **3.** The repeated part of a song coming after each stanza. *pl.* **choruses.**

circumference /sər kum′ fər əns/ *n.* **1.** The boundary line of a circle. **2.** The distance around: *The circumference of the plate is 12 inches.*

civil /siv′ əl/ *adj.* **1.** Having to do with citizens: *civil laws.* **2.** Not naval, military, or connected with the church: *a civil court.* **3.** Polite: *He gave the angry man a civil answer.*

clause /klôz/ *n.* Part of a sentence having a subject and a predicate.

clinic /klin′ ik/ *n.* Place for the medical treatment of certain diseases: *a children's clinic.*

clothe /klōŦH/ *v.* **1.** Put clothes on; provide with clothing: *She was clothed in fine garments for the ceremony.* **2.** Cover: *The trees were clothed in colored leaves.* **clothed** *or* **clad, clothing.**

clothes /klōz/ *n. pl.* Coverings for the body: *The shop has pretty clothes.*

coarse /kôrs/ *or* /kōrs/ *adj.* **1.** Not fine: *coarse sand.* **2.** Rough: *coarse cloth.* **3.** Common; poor; vulgar. **coarser, coarsest.**

cocoa /kō′ kō/ *n.* **1.** Powder made from seeds of the cacao tree. **2.** Drink made from this powder with milk and sugar.

cocoon /kə kün′/ *n.* Silky case spun by caterpillars to live in while they are turning into adult insects: *In spring a moth came out of the cocoon the caterpillar had spun.*

Col. *abbrev.* for *Colonel.*

collide /kə līd′/ *v.* Rush against; hit or strike hard together: *The bus and car collided at the crossroads.* **collided, colliding.** *syn.* **bump; crash.**

collision /kə lizh′ ən/ *n.* **1.** A violent rushing against; hitting or striking hard together: *Two people were killed in the automobile collision.* **2.** Clash; conflict: *a collision of ideas.*

colonel /kėr′ nəl/ *n.* Officer in command of a regiment of soldiers. A colonel ranks next below a general.

colonial /kə lō′ nē əl/ *adj.* Having to do with a colony or colonies; having something to do with the thirteen colonies that became the United States of America.

column /kol′ əm/ *n.* **1.** Slender, upright structure; pillar. **2.** Anything that seems slender and upright like a column: *a column of smoke.* **3.** Narrow division of a page reading from top to bottom. **4.** Part of a newspaper used for a special subject.

combat /kom′ bat/ *n.* Fight; struggle; bat-

/a/ ran /ā/ rain /ã/ care /ä/ car /e/ hen /ē/ he /ėr/ her /i/ in /ī/ ice /o/ not /ō/ no /ô/ off /u/ us
/ū/ use /ü/ tool /ů/ took /ou/ cow /oi/ boy /ch/ church /hw/ when /ng/ sing /sh/ ship /ŦH/ this
/th/ thin /zh/ vision /ə/ about, taken, pencil, lemon, circus

tle: *to be wounded in combat.* /kəm bat′/ *v.* Fight against: *combat the fire.* **combatted, combatting.**

comet /kom′ ət/ *n.* A bright heavenly body with a starlike center and often with a cloudy tail of light. Comets move around the sun in a long oval course.

comfortable /kum′ fərt ə bəl/ *adj.* **1.** Giving comfort: *a comfortable bed.* **2.** At ease; free from pain: *The warm fire made him feel comfortable.*

common /kom′ ən/ *adj.* **1.** Belonging equally to all. **2.** Often met with; familiar: *Snow is common in cold countries.* **3.** Having no special rank: *a common soldier.*

commotion /kə mō′ shən/ *n.* Confusion; disturbance: *The accident caused quite a commotion on the playground.*

compete /kəm pēt′/ *v.* **1.** Try to win: *He was competing against his friend for the spelling prize.* **2.** Take part in a contest: *Will you compete in the race?* **competed, competing.**

compose /kəm pōz′/ *v.* **1.** Make up: *compose a song.* **2.** Make calm: *You must stop crying and compose yourself.* **composed, composing.**

condense /kən dens′/ *v.* **1.** Make denser; become more compact or more strong: *Light is condensed by means of lenses.* **2.** Change from a gas to a liquid. **3.** Put into fewer words: *Condense your report into four lines.* **condensed, condensing.**

conduct /kon′ dukt/ *n.* Way of acting; behavior. /kən dukt′/ *v.* **1.** Direct; manage: *conduct a business.* **2.** Lead an orchestra or a band. **3.** Guide: *conduct a tour through the park.* **4.** Be a channel for: *Metal conducts heat.*

confident /kon′ fə dənt/ *adj.* Certain; sure: *confident of success.*

confusion /kən fū′ zhen/ *n.* **1.** Disorderly condition; tumult. **2.** Mistaking one thing for another: *Words like "believe" sometimes cause confusion in spelling.*

construct /kən strukt′/ *v.* Build; put together; fit together.

contagious /kən tā′ jəs/ *adj.* Easily spreading from one to another; spreading by touch: *Measles is a contagious disease.*

continent /kon′ tə nənt/ *n.* One of the seven great masses of land on the earth. The continents are North America, South America, Europe, Asia, Africa, Australia, and Antarctica.

conversation /kon′ vər sā′ shən/ *n.* Friendly talk; exchange of ideas by talking informally together.

cookbook /kůk′ bůk′/ *n.* Book of recipes.

cooker /kůk′ ər/ *n.* Pot or kettle in which things are cooked.

correction /kə rek′ shən/ *n.* **1.** A setting right: *a correction of his mistake.* **2.** Something put in place of a mistake: *Write your corrections neatly.* **3.** Punishment: *A prison is sometimes called a house of correction.*

cough /kôf/ *v.* Force air from the lungs with sudden effort and noise. —*n.* Act or sound of coughing.

council /koun′ səl/ *n.* Group of people called together to discuss questions and give advice.

counsel /koun′ səl/ *n.* Advice. —*v.* Give advice; recommend. **counseled, counseling.**

countdown /kount′ doun′/ *n.* The calling out of the passing seconds before the launching of a missile or rocket.

counter[1] /koun′ tər/ *n.* **1.** An imitation coin or disk used for counting. **2.** Long table in a store or bank across which goods are given to customers. **3.** Person who counts.

counter[2] /koun′ tər/ *v.* Oppose: *She countered our plan with one of her own.*

cover /kuv′ ər/ *v.* **1.** Put something over. **2.** Be or spread over. **3.** Hide: *cover a mistake.* **4.** Include: *The book covers a year's work in spelling.* **5.** Travel over: *cover 200 miles a day.* —*n.* Anything that protects or hides: *a book cover.*

coward /kou′ ərd/ *n.* A person who lacks courage or is afraid; one who runs from danger; one who is not brave.

crafty /kraf′ tē/ *adj.* Skillful in deceiving others: *The crafty fox lured the rabbit from its hole.* **craftier, craftiest.**

create /krē āt′/ *v.* **1.** Cause to be: *She created a garden in the rocky yard.* **2.** Be the cause of: *create a disturbance.* **created, creating.**

creep /krēp/ *v.* **1.** Crawl; move in a slow, sly

way. **2.** Grow along the ground or over a wall by means of clinging stems: *Ivy has crept over the wall.* **crept, creeping.**

crew /krü/ *n.* **1.** The sailors who work aboard a ship. **2.** The persons who fly and work on an aircraft. **3.** Any group of people working or acting together: *a crew of loggers.* **4.** The members of a rowing team.

cricket[1] /krik′ ət/ *n.* A black insect related to the grasshopper.

cricket[2] /krik′ ət/ *n.* An English outdoor game played with balls, bats, and wickets.

crime /krīm/ *n.* Very wrong deed that is against the law: *Murder is a crime.*

crisis /krī′ sis/ *n.* **1.** Turning point; deciding event. **2.** Time of danger: *The United States faced a crisis after Pearl Harbor.* *pl.* **crises** /krī′ sēz/.

cruise /krüz/ *n.* Pleasure voyage. —*v.* Sail about from place to place. **cruised, cruising.**

cubic /kū′ bik/ *adj.* **1.** Shaped like a cube. **2.** Having length, breadth, and thickness.

cue[1] /kū/ *n.* Hint as to what should be done.

cue[2] /kū/ *n.* Long stick used for striking a ball in the game of billiards or pool.

curb /kėrb/ *v.* Restrain; hold back: *Curb your laughter.* —*n.* **1.** Check; restraint: *a curb on expenses.* **2.** A raised concrete or stone border along the edge of a pavement or sidewalk.

custom /kus′ təm/ *n.* **1.** A usual action; habit. **2.** A long-established habit that has almost the force of law. **customs** *n. pl.* **1.** Taxes paid to the government on things brought in from a foreign country. **2.** The office where such imported things are checked.

Dd

daily /dā′ lē/ *adj.* Done, happening, or appearing every day. —*adv.* Day by day. —*n.* Newspaper printed every day. *pl.* **dailies.**

dairy /dãr′ ē/ *n.* **1.** Place where milk and cream are kept and made into butter and cheese. **2.** Store or company that sells milk, butter, cream, and cheese. *pl.* **dairies.**

damp /damp/ *adj.* Slightly wet; moist. —*n.* Moisture: *We could feel the damp in the air.*

dauntless /dônt′ ləs/ *adj.* Brave; not able to be frightened or discouraged.

debate /dē bāt′/ *v.* Talk about reasons for and against. **debated, debating.** —*n.* Discussion of reasons for and against.

decade /dek′ ād/ *n.* Ten years: *From 1910 to 1920 was a decade.*

deceive /dē sēv′/ *v.* Lie; use deceit; make a person believe something to be true that is false. **deceived, deceiving.**

declare /dē klãr′/ *v.* Say; make known. **declared, declaring.**

decline /dē klīn′/ *v.* **1.** Refuse; turn away from doing. **2.** Refuse politely: *decline an invitation.* **3.** Bend or slope. **4.** Grow less in strength and power. **declined, declining.** —*n.* **1.** A losing of strength; a growing worse. **2.** The last part: *the decline of the day.*

decoy /dē koi′/ *v.* Lead into danger by means of trickery: *We will decoy the criminals and capture them.* /dē′ koi/ *n.* Artificial bird used to lure birds into a trap or near a hunter: *The decoy was lost in the lake.*

decrease /dē krēs′/ *v.* Grow, become, or make less. **decreased, decreasing.** /dē′ krēs/ *n.* Amount by which a thing becomes less: *The decrease in heat was ten degrees.*

deem /dēm/ *v.* Think; believe; consider: *I do not deem it wise to have a picnic today.*

defense /dē fens′/ *n.* **1.** Any thing, act, or word that defends, guards, or protects. **2.** Act of defending: *his defense of Tom's speech.* **3.** A defending team: *a team or players defending a goal in a game.*

dent /dent/ *n.* Hollow made by a blow or pressure: *The fallen limb made a dent in her car.* —*v.* **1.** Make a dent in. **2.** Become dented.

dentist /den′ tist/ *n.* Doctor whose work is the care of the teeth.

/a/ ran /ā/ rain /ã/ care /ä/ car /e/ hen /ē/ he /ėr/ her /i/ in /ī/ ice /o/ not /ō/ no /ô/ off /u/ us /ū/ use /ü/ tool /ù/ took /ou/ cow /oi/ boy /ch/ church /hw/ when /ng/ sing /sh/ ship /ᴛʜ/ this /th/ thin /zh/ vision /ə/ about, taken, pencil, lemon, circus

deny /dē nī′/ v. **1.** Say something is not true. **2.** Say that one does not accept. **3.** Refuse. **denied, denying.**

depart /dē pärt′/ v. **1.** Go away; leave. **2.** Change: *Do not depart from your usual way of working.* **3.** Die.

dependable /dē pen′ də bəl/ adj. Reliable; trustworthy.

dependent /dē pen′ dənt/ adj. Trusting another person or thing for help: *He is dependent on his parents for support.* —n. Person who is supported by another.

depression /dē presh′ ən/ n. **1.** A pressing down; a hollow: *depressions in the ground.* **2.** Low feeling; sadness: *The picnic cured the boy's depression.*

descend /dē send′/ v. **1.** Come or go down from a higher place to a lower place: *We descended the mountain.* **2.** Slope downward. **3.** Be handed down from parent to child.

despair /də spãr′/ n. Loss of all hope. —v. Lose all hope; be without hope: *despair of saving the child's life.*

despise /dē spīz′/ v. Look down on; feel contempt for: *We despise liars.* **despised, despising.**

dessert /də zərt′/ n. Sweets at the end of a meal: *Father likes apple pie for dessert.*

detect /dē tekt′/ v. Find out; discover: *Can you detect the odor of smoke in the room.*

dictate /dik′ tāt/ v. **1.** Make others do what one says. **2.** Say or read something for another person or persons to write down: *dictate a sentence.* **dictated, dictating.**

disagreeable /dis′ ə grē′ ə bəl/ adj. **1.** Not pleasant: *Rainy weather is disagreeable.* **2.** Unfriendly; unkind: *a disagreeable person.*

discard /dis kärd′/ v. Throw aside; give up as useless: *discard old clothes; discard a bad habit.*

discharge /dis chärj′/ v. **1.** Unload passengers. **2.** Shoot: *discharge a gun.* **3.** Dismiss. **4.** Pay (a debt). **5.** Perform (a duty). **discharged, discharging.** /dis′ chärj/ n. A release; a letting go; a dismissing: *a discharge from the army.*

discussion /dis kush′ ən/ n. A going over things for and against; discussing things; talk.

disgust /dis gust′/ n. Strong dislike: *We feel disgust for a bad odor.* —v. Arouse disgust in: *The smell of a pigpen disgusts many people.*

dismiss /dis mis′/ v. **1.** Send away; allow to go: *The class was dismissed at noon.* **2.** Remove from office or service: *They were dismissed from their jobs for laziness.*

disturbance /dis tėr′ bəns/ n. **1.** A destroying of peace, quiet, or rest. **2.** A thing that destroys peace, quiet, or rest.

dodge /doj/ v. **1.** Move quickly to one side. **2.** Move quickly to get away from. **3.** Get away from by some trick: *He dodged all the questions.* **dodged, dodging.**

donate /dō′ nāt/ v. Give; contribute. **donated, donating.**

doughnut /dō′ nut′/ n. Small, sweet cake cooked in deep fat. Doughnuts are usually made in the shape of a ring.

downfall /doun′ fôl′/ n. **1.** Sudden overthrow or ruin. **2.** Heavy fall of rain or snow.

drawback /drô′ bak′/ n. Disadvantage: *The rainy weather was a drawback on our trip.*

drawbridge /drô′ brij′/ n. Bridge that can be lifted or partly lifted or moved to one side.

dreary /drir′ ē/ adj. Dull; gloomy; cheerless; depressing. **drearier, dreariest.**

drive /drīv/ v. **1.** Make go. **2.** Manage or operate successfully. **3.** Go or carry in a car. **drove, driven, driving.** —n. Special effort: *a Red Cross drive for funds.*

driven /driv′ ən/ v. See **drive.** *We were driven to the airport by my uncle.*

driveway /drīv′ wā′/ n. Road to drive on, often leading from a house or garage to the public road.

drought /drout/ n. **1.** Long period of dry weather. **2.** Lack of water; dryness.

drowsy /drou′ zē/ adj. **1.** Sleepy. **2.** Causing sleepiness. **drowsier, drowsiest.**

drumstick /drum′ stik′/ n. **1.** Stick for beating a drum. **2.** Lower half of the leg of a cooked chicken or turkey.

duet /dü et′/ n. **1.** Piece of music for two voices or instruments. **2.** Two singers or players performing together.

dune /dūn/ *n.* Mound or ridge of loose sand heaped up by the wind.

Ee

eager /ē′ gər/ *adj.* Wanting very much; desiring very strongly: *The eager scholar studied long hours to learn French.*

earache /ir′ āk′/ *n.* Pain in the ear.

earring /ir′ ring′/ *n.* Ornament for the ear.

elect /ē lekt′/ *v.* **1.** Choose by voting for an office: *elect a senator.* **2.** Choose: *I elected to go.* —*adj.* Chosen; selected.

elevator /el′ ə vā′ tər/ *n.* **1.** Moving platform or cage to carry persons or things up and down in a building or mine. **2.** Building for storing grain. **3.** Movable, flat piece of the tail of an airplane to cause it to go up or down.

embroider /em broi′ dər/ *v.* **1.** Ornament cloth or leather with a design or pattern of stitches. **2.** Make a design or pattern on cloth or leather. **3.** Do embroidery. **4.** Add imaginary details.

employer /em ploi′ ər/ *n.* Person or firm that gives work and pay to people.

employment /em ploi′ mənt/ *n.* **1.** A person's work. **2.** Job; work.

enable /en ā′ bəl/ *v.* Make able; give power or means to: *Airplanes enable us to travel rapidly.* **enabled, enabling.**

endless /end′ ləs/ *adj.* **1.** Having no end. **2.** Never stopping; going on and on.

engage /en gāj′/ *v.* **1.** Take part: *engage in an activity.* **2.** Occupy: *Work engages their attention all day.* **3.** Promise to marry: *He is engaged to my sister.* **engaged, engaging.**

enjoyable /en joi′ ə bəl/ *adj.* Giving joy; pleasant; able to be enjoyed: *The class agreed that the circus was enjoyable.*

enlarge /en lärj′/ *v.* **1.** Make larger. **2.** Grow larger. **enlarged, enlarging.**

enlargement /en lärj′ mənt/ *n.* Anything that is a larger form of something else.

entire /en tīr′/ *adj.* Having all the parts or elements; whole; complete.

envy /en′ vē/ *n.* **1.** Feeling of ill will at another's good fortune. **2.** Feeling of dislike or desire because another has what one wants. —*v.* Feel ill will toward another person because of what the person has. **envies, envied, envying.**

erupt /ē rupt′/ *v.* **1.** Burst forth: *Lava erupted from the volcano.* **2.** Come out: *The child's teeth erupted.*

evidence /ev′ ə dəns/ *n.* Facts; proof; anything that shows or makes clear: *The jam on his face was evidence that he had been in the kitchen.* —*v.* Show clearly: *Her smile evidenced her pleasure.* **evidenced, evidencing.**

evil /ē′ vəl/ *adj.* Bad; wrong; causing harm: *an evil person; an evil deed.* —*n.* Thing causing harm.

ex— *prefix.* **1.** Out: *Export* means *carry out.* **2.** Former: *Ex-president* means *former president.*

excellent /ek′ sə lənt/ *adj.* Extremely good; better than others: *Excellent work deserves high praise.*

exhale /eks hāl′/ *v.* Breathe out: *We exhale air from the lungs.* **exhaled, exhaling.**

existence /eg zis′ təns/ *n.* **1.** Being: *come into existence.* **2.** Being real: *the existence of ghosts.* **3.** Life: *a happy existence.*

exit /ek′ sit/ *n.* **1.** Way out: *The school has four exits.* **2.** Act of leaving the stage. —*v.* Go out; depart; leave the stage.

explode /ek splōd′/ *v.* **1.** Blow up; burst. **2.** Cause to blow up or burst. **3.** Burst forth noisily: *explode into laughter.* **exploded, exploding.**

export /eks′ pôrt/ or /ek spôrt′/ *v.* Send goods out of one's country for sale and use in another: *The United States exports automobiles.* /eks′ pôrt/ *n.* Article exported: *Cotton is an export of the United States.*

/a/ ran /ā/ rain /ā/ care /ä/ car /e/ hen /ē/ he /ėr/ her /i/ in /ī/ ice /o/ not /ō/ no /ô/ off /u/ us /ū/ use /ü/ tool /u̇/ took /ou/ cow /oi/ boy /ch/ church /hw/ when /ng/ sing /sh/ ship /ŦH/ this /th/ thin /zh/ vision /ə/ about, taken, pencil, lemon, circus

Ff

fable /fā′ bəl/ *n.* **1.** Story that is made up to teach a lesson: *"The Hare and the Tortoise" is a fable.* **2.** Story that is not true: *Her story about a summer trip is just a fable.*

fact /fakt/ *n.* **1.** Thing known to be true: *It is a fact that Columbus discovered America in 1492.* **2.** Thing said or supposed to be true: *We doubted those facts.*

fair¹ /fãr/ *adj.* **1.** Not favoring one or the other; honest: *a fair trial.* **2.** According to the rules: *a fair game.* **3.** Pretty good; average: *The movie was only fair.* **4.** Light; not dark: *fair skin.* **5.** Not cloudy: *fair weather.* —*adv.* In a fair manner: *I believe in playing fair.*

fair² /fãr/ *or* /fer/ *n.* **1.** A showing of products and manufactured goods to help people see what has been done and to urge them to buy better seed, stock, and machinery: *a state fair.* **2.** A showing and sale of articles, often for charity: *a book fair.*

falsehood /fôls′ hùd′/ *n.* Lie; untruth; false statement.

farmhouse /färm′ hous′/ *n.* House to live in on a farm.

fatal /fā′ təl/ *adj.* **1.** Causing death: *a fatal accident.* **2.** Causing ruin: *The rain was fatal to our picnic.* **3.** Important; fateful: *At last the fatal day of the test arrived.*

faucet /fô′ sət/ *n.* Device for turning off the flow of water or other liquid from a pipe or container.

faultless /fôlt′ ləs/ *adj.* Without a single fault; perfect.

fearful /fir′ fəl/ *adj.* **1.** Terrible; dreadful. **2.** Feeling fear; frightened. **3.** Showing fear.

feast /fēst/ *n.* Rich meal for a special occasion; banquet. —*v.* Eat a rich meal; provide a rich meal for.

fertile /fėr′ təl/ *adj.* **1.** Able to bear fruit, seeds, or young: *a fertile plant or animal.* **2.** Able to develop into a new individual: *Chicks hatch from fertile eggs.* **3.** Able to produce much: *fertile soil.*

fierce /firs/ *adj.* Savage; wild. **fiercer, fiercest.**

film /film/ *n.* **1.** Very thin coating: *a film of oil on the water.* **2.** Roll of material used to take photographs: *film for a camera.* **3.** Motion picture: *a film about animals.* —*v.* **1.** Cover with a film. **2.** Make a motion picture of.

final /fī′ nəl/ *adj.* Coming last: *the final chapter of a book.*

finger /fing′ gər/ *n.* One of the five parts of the hand, especially the four beside the thumb.

fingerprint /fing′ gər print′/ *n.* Markings or impression of markings on inner surface of the end of a finger. —*v.* Take fingerprints of.

fireplace /fīr′ plās′/ *n.* Place built to hold a fire.

fishhook /fish′ hùk′/ *n.* Hook for catching fish.

flaw /flô/ *n.* Slight defect; fault.

flesh /flesh/ *n.* **1.** The soft substance of the body that covers the bones and is covered by skin. **2.** Meat. **3.** The soft part of fruits or vegetables: *The flesh of a peach is a pale yellow.*

flood /flud/ *v.* **1.** Fill to overflowing. **2.** Flow over. —*n.* Flow of water over usually dry land.

flue /flü/ *n.* A passage for smoke or hot air: *A chimney often has several flues.*

fluid /flü′ əd/ *n.* Any liquid or gas; something that will flow. —*adj.* **1.** Like a fluid: *She poured the fluid mass of hot candy into a dish to harden.* **2.** Changing easily; not fixed or firm: *a fluid situation.*

foil¹ /foil/ *v.* Prevent from carrying out plans, attempts, etc.; get the better of.

foil² /foil/ *n.* Metal beaten or rolled into a very thin sheet: *Candy is sometimes wrapped in foil.*

foil³ /foil/ *n.* A long, narrow sword used in fencing.

folder /fōl′ dər/ *n.* A holder for papers, made of stiff paper doubled once.

foolish /fü′ lish/ *adj.* **1.** Lacking in good sense or judgment. **2.** Like a fool; silly.

foolproof /fül′ prüf′/ *adj.* So safe or simple that even a fool can use or do it.

footstep /fùt′ step′/ *n.* **1.** A person's step. **2.** Distance covered in one step. **3.** Sound of steps coming.

footstool /fut′ stül′/ *n.* Low stool on which to place the feet when seated.

forbid /fôr′ bid′/ *v.* Not allow; make a rule against: *The teacher forbade us to leave our seats.* **forbad** or **forebade, forbidden** or **forbid, forbidding.**

forearm /fôr′ ärm′/ *n.* The part of the arm between the wrist and the elbow.

forecast /fôr′ kast/ *v.* Predict; tell what is coming: *Cooler weather is forecast for tomorrow.* **forecast** or **forecasted, forecasting.** —*n.* Prediction: *What is the forecast for tomorrow?*

form /fôrm/ *n.* **1.** Shape. **2.** Kind; sort: *Snow is a form of water.* **3.** Arrangement: *The test was in the form of sentences.* **4.** Mold. —*v.* **1.** Shape. **2.** Become: *Ice formed on the pond.* **3.** Develop: *form good habits.*

former /fôr′mər/ *adj.* **1.** The first of two: *Canada and the United States are in North America; Montreal is in the former country.* **2.** Earlier; past: *former years.*

fragrance /frā′ grəns/ *n.* Sweet smell.

frail /frāl/ *adj.* Delicate and not very strong; weak: *That frail plant cannot live outdoors in cold weather.*

freckle /frek′ əl/ *n.* Small, light-brown spot that some people have on the skin. —*v.* Become marked or spotted with freckles. **freckled, freckling.**

freedom /frē′ dəm/ *n.* **1.** Being free. **2.** Liberty; power to do, say, or think as one pleases.

freeway /frē′ wā′/ *n.* A multilane, toll-free expressway with access only at established points.

fruitcake /früt′ kāk′/ *n.* Cake made with fruits, nuts, etc., and often served at holidays.

funnel /fun′ əl/ *n.* **1.** Open vessel ending at the bottom in a tube. **2.** Anything shaped like a funnel. **3.** Smokestack or chimney on a steamship or steam engine.

furnish /fėr′ nish/ *v.* **1.** Supply; provide: *furnish an army with blankets.* **2.** Supply with furniture: *furnish a bedroom.*

furthermore /fėr′ ᴛʜər môr′/ *adv.* Moreover; also; besides.

Gg

gadget /gaj′ ət/ *n.* Small device or contrivance: *Can openers are kitchen gadgets.*

gale /gāl/ *n.* A very strong wind.

galley /gal′ ē/ *n.* **1.** Long, narrow ship of former times having oars and sails. **2.** The kitchen of a ship. *pl.* **galleys.**

gaunt /gônt/ *adj.* Very thin and bony, with hollow eyes and a starved look: *Hunger had made him gaunt.*

gleam /glēm/ *v.* Shine; shine brightly. —*n.* A bright beam of light: *the gleam of headlights.*

glimpse /glimps/ *n.* Very brief view; short look: *I got a glimpse of the falls as our train went by.* —*v.* Catch a brief view of: *I glimpsed her dress as she went by.* **glimpsed, glimpsing.**

gloomy /glüm′ ē/ *adj.* **1.** Dark; dim: *a gloomy winter day.* **2.** Sad: *She is in a gloomy mood.* **3.** Discouraging: *a gloomy predicament.* **gloomier, gloomiest.**

graceful /grās′ fəl/ *adj.* Having beauty of form or movement: *a graceful dancer.*

grammar /gram′ ər/ *n.* **1.** The study of the forms and uses of words. **2.** The rules about the uses of words. **3.** Use of words according to rules: *good grammar.*

grocer /grō′ sər/ *n.* Person who sells food and household supplies.

groove /grüv/ *n.* **1.** Long, narrow cut or furrow; rut. **2.** Fixed way of doing things. —*v.* Make a cut, rut, or narrow channel with a tool. **grooved, grooving.**

grouchy /grou′ chē/ *adj.* Sulky; sullen; discontented. **grouchier, grouchiest.**

growth /grōth/ *n.* **1.** Development. **2.** Amount grown: *one year's growth.*

/a/ ran /ā/ rain /â/ care /ä/ car /e/ hen /ē/ he /ėr/ her /i/ in /ī/ ice /o/ not /ō/ no /ô/ off /u/ us
/ū/ use /ü/ tool /ù/ took /ou/ cow /oi/ boy /ch/ church /hw/ when /ng/ sing /sh/ ship /ᴛʜ/ this
/th/ thin /zh/ vision /ə/ about, taken, pencil, lemon, circus

Hh

handcuff /hand′ kuf′/ *n.* Device to keep persons from using their hands, usually one of two steel bracelets joined by a short chain and fastened around the wrists. —*v.* Put handcuffs on.

hangar /hang′ ər/ *n.* Shed for airplanes or airships.

hardship /härd′ ship′/ *n.* Something hard to bear; hard living conditions.

harpoon /här pün′/ *n.* Spear with rope tied to it used for catching sea animals. —*v.* Strike, catch, or kill by using a harpoon.

harsh /härsh/ *adj.* **1.** Rough to the touch, taste, eye, or ear: *a harsh voice.* **2.** Cruel; unfeeling; severe: *a harsh leader.*

harvest /här′ vəst/ *v.* Gather in and bring home for use. —*n.* **1.** Reaping and gathering in of food crops. **2.** Time or season of the harvest. **3.** Result; consequences: *He is reaping the harvest of his mistakes.*

hatchet /hat′ chət/ *n.* Small ax with a handle about a foot long, for use with one hand.

hatred /hā′ trəd/ *n.* Great dislike; hate.

hawk /hôk/ *n.* Bird of prey with a strong, hooked beak, long claws, and broad wings.

hazardous /haz′ ərd əs/ *adj.* Dangerous; risky.

headache /hed′ āk′/ *n.* A pain in the head.

heed /hēd/ *v.* Give careful attention to; take notice of: *Please heed what I say.*

heedless /hēd′ ləs/ *adj.* Careless; thoughtless.

height /hīt/ *n.* **1.** Measurement from top to bottom; how high anything is. **2.** A fairly great distance up.

hew /hū/ *v.* Cut; chop with an ax. **hewed, hewn** or **hewed, hewing.**

highlight /hī′ līt′/ *n.* The most important or interesting part: *The highlight of the picnic was the swimming match.* —*v.* **1.** Put attention on; mark for special attention. **2.** Cast a bright light on; make bright. **highlighted, highlighting.**

hoard /hôrd/ *v.* Save and store away: *Squirrels hoard nuts for the winter.* —*n.* What is saved and stored away: *The squirrel's hoard was kept in a tree.*

hoarse /hôrs/ *adj.* **1.** Sounding rough and deep: *a hoarse voice.* **2.** Having a rough voice. **hoarser, hoarsest.**

hoax /hōks/ *n.* A trick, especially a made-up story passed off as true; a cruel joke. *pl.* **hoaxes.**

hobble /hob′ əl/ *v.* **1.** Limp. **2.** Tie the legs of a horse together: *The horse was hobbled so that it would not run away.* **hobbled, hobbling.** —*n.* Rope or strap used to tie a horse's legs together.

hobby /hob′ ē/ *n.* Something a person especially likes to do or study that is not his or her main business. *pl.* **hobbies.**

hockey /hok′ ē/ *n.* Game played by two teams on ice or on a field. Ice hockey is played on an ice rink by two teams of six players on skates. The object of the game is to put a round rubber disk, called the puck, into the opponents goal with a hockey stick.

holy /hō′ lē/ *adj.* **1.** Belonging to God; sacred. **2.** Like a saint. **3.** Worthy of reverence. **holier, holiest.**

honey /hun′ ē/ *n.* Thick, sweet, yellow liquid made by bees.

hopscotch /hop′ skoch′/ *n.* Game played by jumping into or across numbered squares.

horror /hôr′ ər/ *n.* Terror; very strong dislike: *The child had a horror of snakes.*

hostile /hos′ təl/ *or* /hos′ tīl/ *adj.* **1.** Of an enemy: *the hostile army.* **2.** Opposed; unfriendly; unfavorable.

however /hou′ ev′ ər/ *conj.* Nevertheless; inspite of all that.

humane /hū mān′/ *adj.* Kind; not cruel or brutal: *humane treatment of animals.*

humid /hū′ mid/ *adj.* Moist; damp.

humorous /hū′ mər əs/ *adj.* Funny; amusing: *a humorous story.*

hunger /hung′ gər/ *n.* Desire or need for food. —*v.* Feel hunger for: *She hungers for a friend.*

hurdle /hėr′ dəl/ *n.* **1.** Barrier for people or horses to jump over in a race. **2.** Obstacle; difficulty. —*v.* Jump over: *The horse hurdled the fence easily.* **hurdled, hurdling.**

husky /hus′ kē/ *adj.* **1.** Dry in the throat; hoarse. **2.** Big and strong. **huskier, huskiest.**

hymn /him/ *n.* Song in praise or honor of God; any song of praise.

Ii

iceberg /īs′ bėrg′/ *n.* Large mass of ice floating in the sea.

idle /ī′ dəl/ *adj.* **1.** Doing nothing; not busy; not working. **2.** Lazy; not willing to do things. **3.** Worthless; useless: *idle pleasures.* **idler, idlest.** *ant.* **busy.** —*v.* Be idle; do nothing. **idled, idling.**

idol /ī′ dəl/ *n.* **1.** Image that is worshiped as a god. **2.** Person or thing that is loved very much: *The baby was the idol of the family.*

igloo /ig′ lü/ *n.* An Eskimo hut that is shaped like a dome and is often made of blocks of hard snow. *pl.* **igloos.**

ignorance /ig′ nə rəns/ *n.* Lack of knowledge; being ignorant.

ignorant /ig′ nə rənt/ *adj.* Knowing little or nothing.

ignore /ig nôr′/ *v.* Pay no attention to; disregard: *The driver ignored the policeman's whistle.* **ignored, ignoring.**

illness /il′ nəs/ *n.* Sickness; poor health. *pl.* **illnesses.**

immigrant /im′ ə grənt/ *n.* Person who comes to live in a country or region: *Canada has many immigrants from Europe.*

impeachment /im pēch′ mənt/ *n.* Act of accusing a public official of wrong conduct before a court of justice.

import /im′ pôrt/ *n.* **1.** Article brought into a country from another. **2.** Importance: *matters of great import.* /im pôrt′/ *v.* Bring an article or articles into a country for sale or use.

impossible /im pos′ ə bəl/ *adj.* Not possible to use; not to be done: *Few things are impossible.*

impress /im pres′/ *v.* **1.** Have a strong effect on the mind or feelings of. **2.** Fix in the mind. **3.** Make marks on by pressing or stamping.

improvement /im prüv′ mənt/ *n.* **1.** Making or becoming better: *His school work shows improvement.* **2.** Change that adds value: *improvement in his house.* **3.** Better condition: *Automobiles are an improvement over horses.*

in— *prefix.* **1.** Not: *Inexpensive* means *not expensive.* **2.** The opposite of: *Inattention* means *the opposite of attention.*

increase /in krēs′/ *v.* **1.** Make greater, more powerful, richer, etc. **2.** Become greater: *Our wealth increased.* **increased, increasing.** /in′ krēs/ *n.* Gain; growth: *an increase in school enrollment.*

independence /in′ də pen′ dəns/ *n.* Freedom from the control, help, or support of others: *The colonies won independence from England.*

industrious /in dus′ trē əs/ *adj.* Hard-working: *An industrious student usually gets good grades.*

inflict /in flikt′/ *v.* Impose or give something unwelcome: *The cruel tyrant inflicted harsh punishments for disobedience.*

inhale /in hāl′/ *v.* Draw into the lungs; breathe in. **inhaled, inhaling.**

innocent /in′ ə sənt/ *adj.* **1.** Doing no wrong; not guilty. **2.** Without knowledge of evil: *A baby is innocent.* **3.** Doing no harm: *innocent pleasures.*

install /in stôl′/ *v.* **1.** Place in office with certain ceremonies. **2.** Put in position for use: *The telephone was installed on Friday.*

instruction /in struk′ shən/ *n.* Teaching; education; knowledge.

introduction /in′ trə duk′ shən/ *n.* **1.** An introducing. **2.** The beginning of a speech, book, piece of music, etc. **3.** Being introduced: *She was shy at her introduction to the company.*

invisible /in viz′ ə bəl/ *adj.* Not visible; not able to be seen: *Oxygen is invisible.*

issue /ish′ ü/ *v.* **1.** Send out: *The magazine is issued once a month.* **2.** Come out: *Smoke*

/a/ ran /ā/ rain /ã/ care /ä/ car /e/ hen /ē/ he /ėr/ her /i/ in /ī/ ice /o/ not /ō/ no /ô/ off /u/ us
/ū/ use /ü/ tool /u̇/ took /ou/ cow /oi/ boy /ch/ church /hw/ when /ng/ sing /sh/ ship /ᴛʜ/ this
/th/ thin /zh/ vision /ə/ about, taken, pencil, lemon, circus

issues from a chimney. **issued, issuing.** *—n.* **1.** Something sent out: *The last issue of the paper came out on Monday.* **2.** Point to be debated. **3.** Problem.

Jj

jeer /jir/ *v.* Make fun in a rude or unkind way. *—n.* A mocking or insulting remark.

jersey /jėr′zē/ *n.* **1.** Close-fitting sweater. **2.** Knitted cloth made by a machine. *pl.* **jerseys.**

jewel /jü′əl/ *n.* **1.** Precious stone; stone of great value. **2.** A valuable ornament to be worn, set with precious stones. **3.** Person or thing that is very precious. *—v.* Set with jewels.

jigsaw /jig′sô′/ *n.* Narrow saw mounted in a frame and worked with an up-and-down motion, used to cut curves.

jockey /jok′ē/ *n.* Person who rides horses in races. *pl.* **jockeys.**

judge /juj/ *n.* **1.** A government official appointed or elected to hear and decide cases in a law court. **2.** Person chosen to settle a dispute, decide who wins a race, etc. **3.** Person who can decide on how good a thing is. *—v.* **1.** Hear and decide a case in a law court. **2.** Form an opinion about. **3.** Settle a dispute, decide who wins a race, etc. **4.** Criticize; blame. **judged, judging.**

juice /jüs/ *or* /jūs/ *n.* **1.** Liquid parts of fruits, vegetables, and meats. **2.** Liquids in the body: *the juices of the stomach.* *—v.* To supply with juice. **juiced, juicing.**

Kk

kernel /kėr′nəl/ *n.* **1.** A grain or seed like that of wheat or corn. **2.** The central or important part of anything, around which it is formed or built up.

knapsack /nap′sak′/ *n.* A leather or canvas bag for clothes, equipment, etc., carried on the back.

knew /nū/ *or* /nü/ *v.* See **know.** *He knew the answer.*

knot /not/ *n.* **1.** A twining or tying together of parts of one or more ropes, strings, etc. **2.** Measure of speed used on ships. *—v.* **1.** Tie or fasten parts of string together. **2.** Tangle. **knotted, knotting.**

know /nō/ *v.* **1.** Have the facts of; be skilled in. **2.** Be acquainted with. **knew, known, knowing.**

known /nōn/ *v.* See **know.** *He was known for his artistic ability.*

Ll

labor /lā′bər/ *n.* Work; toil: *He was well paid for the labor.* *—v.* **1.** Work hard: *They labored to plow the field.* **2.** Move slowly and heavily: *The car labored up the steep hill.*

laughter /laf′tər/ *n.* The action of laughing; the sound of laughter.

laundry /lôn′drē/ *n.* **1.** Room or building where clothes are washed and ironed. **2.** Clothes washed or to be washed. *pl.* **laundries.**

lawnmower /lôn′mō′ər/ *n.* Machine with revolving blades for cutting the grass on a lawn.

lawyer /lô′yər/ *n.* Person who knows the laws and gives advice about matters of law or acts for another person in court.

leather /leᴛн′ər/ *n.* Material made from the skin of an animal by removing the hairs and then tanning it: *Shoes are made of leather.* *—adj.* Made of leather: *leather gloves.*

legal /lē′gəl/ *adj.* **1.** Of law: *legal advice.* **2.** Lawful: *Hunting is legal during the official hunting season.*

liar /lī′ər/ *n.* Person who tells lies; person who says what is not true.

likewise /līk′wīz′/ *adv.* **1.** The same: *See what I do; I hope you do likewise.* **2.** Also: *I must go home, and she likewise.*

linen /lin′ən/ *n.* **1.** Cloth or thread made from flax. **2.** Articles made of linen or some substitute. *—adj.* Made of linen: *linen napkins.*

liquid /lik′wid/ *n.* Substance that is not a

solid or a gas; substance that flows freely, like water. —*adj.* In liquid form; melted.

local /lō′ kəl/ *adj.* **1.** Of a place; having to do with a certain place or places: *local news.* **2.** Of just one part of the body: *a local pain.*

locate /lō′ kāt/ *v.* **1.** Establish in a place. **2.** Find out the exact position of. **3.** State or show the exact position of: *locate Africa on the globe.* **located, locating.**

location /lō kā′ shən/ *n.* **1.** A locating: *the location of the camp.* **2.** A being located. **3.** Position; place: *a bad location.*

loiter /loi′ tər/ *v.* Linger idly; stop and play along the way.

lore /lôr/ *n.* The facts and stories about a certain subject: *fairy lore; Greek lore.*

lowland /lō′ land′/ *n.* Land that is lower and flatter than the other land around it.

loyal /loi′ əl/ *adj.* **1.** True and faithful to love, promise, or duty. **2.** Faithful to one's kind, government, or country: *a loyal citizen.*

lucky /luk′ ē/ *adj.* Having or bringing good luck: *a lucky day.* **luckier, luckiest.**

lunar /lü′ nər/ *adj.* Of the moon: *a lunar eclipse.*

Mm

magic /maj′ ik/ *n.* The pretended art of making things happen by secret charms and sayings. —*adj.* Done as if by secret charms: *A magic palace stood in place of the woodcutter's hut.*

mainland /mān′ land′/ *n.* The main part of a continent apart from the outlying islands.

maintain /mān tān′/ *v.* **1.** Keep up; keep in existence; carry on: *maintain a business.* **2.** Declare to be true: *He maintained that he was innocent.*

major /mā′ jər/ *adj.* Larger; greater: *The major part of a baby's life is spent sleeping.* —*n.* An officer in the army, ranking next above a captain.

majority /mə jôr′ ə tē/ *n.* The larger number; more than half: *A majority of the children have read that book.* *pl.* **majorities.**

manual /man′ ū əl/ *n.* Small book of explanations. —*adj.* Done with the hands: *manual labor.*

margin /mär′ jən/ *n.* **1.** Edge; border. **2.** The blank space around the writing or printing on a page. **3.** An extra amount: *We allow a margin of 15 minutes to catch the bus.*

maroon[1] /mə rün′/ *adj.* Very dark, brownish red: *a maroon coat.*

maroon[2] /mə rün′/ *v.* Leave in a lonely, helpless position: *The shipwrecked crew was marooned on the island.*

massive /mas′ iv/ *adj.* **1.** Forming a large mass; huge: *a massive rock.* **2.** In great numbers; extensive: *a massive crowd.* **3.** Imposing; impressive.

matchless /mach′ ləs/ *adj.* So great or wonderful that it cannot be equaled: *The firemen showed matchless courage.*

material /mə tir′ ē əl/ *n.* What a thing is made from or done with: *dress material; writing materials.* —*adj.* Of the body: *Food and shelter are material needs.*

mattress /mat′ rəs/ *n.* Covering of strong cloth stuffed with cotton, straw, etc., used on a bed or as a bed. A spring mattress contains wire springs. *pl.* **mattresses.**

mayor /mā′ ər/ *n.* Person at the head of a city or town government.

measles /mē′ zəlz/ *n.* An infectious disease characterized by cold, fever, and a breaking out of small red spots.

mechanical /mə kan′ ə kəl/ *adj.* **1.** Having to do with machinery. **2.** Worked by machinery: *a mechanical toy.* **3.** Without expression: *Their singing was very mechanical.*

melon /mel′ ən/ *n.* Large, juicy fruit of the vine.

member /mem′ bər/ *n.* **1.** One who belongs to a group. **2.** Part of a plant, animal, or human body, especially an arm or a leg.

/a/ ran /ā/ rain /ā/ care /ä/ car /e/ hen /ē/ he /ėr/ her /i/ in /ī/ ice /o/ not /ō/ no /ô/ off /u/ us
/ū/ use /ü/ tool /ù/ took /ou/ cow /oi/ boy /ch/ church /hw/ when /ng/ sing /sh/ ship /ŦH/ this
/th/ thin /zh/ vision /ə/ about, taken, pencil, lemon, circus

mercy /mėr′sē/ *n.* **1.** More kindness than is called for or expected. **2.** A blessing: *It's a mercy you weren't injured. pl.* **mercies.**

mere /mir/ *adj.* Nothing else than; only: *a mere scratch.*

merge /mėrj/ *v.* **1.** Swallow up; combine; absorb: *The big company merged several small businesses.* **2.** Become swallowed up: *Day merged into night.* **merged, merging.**

meter[1] /mē′tər/ *n.* **1.** Measure of length equal to about 39½ inches. **2.** Kind of poetic rhythm. **3.** The time arrangement in music.

meter[2] /mē′tər/ *n.* Something that measures or measures and records: *a water meter.*

method /meth′əd/ *n.* **1.** Way of doing something. **2.** System of doing things.

metric /met′rik/ *adj.* Belonging to a system of measurement which counts by ten: *the metric system.*

minor /mī′nər/ *adj.* Smaller; less important. —*n.* Person under the age of responsibility, usually under 21 years. *syn.* **lesser; inferior.**

miser /mī′zər/ *n.* Person who loves money for its own sake and lives poorly in order to save money.

missile /mis′əl/ *n.* **1.** Object that is thrown, hurled, or shot. **2.** A rocket used in warfare.

mistreat /mis trēt′/ *v.* Treat badly.

mistrust /mis trust′/ *v.* Feel no confidence in; doubt. —*n.* Lack of trust.

moisten /mois′ən/ *v.* Make or become moist: *Her eyes moistened with tears.*

moisture /mois′chər/ *n.* Slight wetness. Dew is moisture that collects on grass at night.

molar /mō′lər/ *n.* Tooth with a broad surface for grinding having somewhat flattened points. The twelve permanent back teeth in human beings are molars.

mold[1] /mōld/ *n.* A hollow shape in which anything is formed to that shape. —*v.* Make or form into a shape.

mold[2] /mōld/ *n.* A furry growth that appears on vegetable and animal substances left too long in a warm, moist place. —*v.* Become covered with mold.

mold[3] /mōld/ *n.* Loose earth; fine, soft, rich earth: *Wild flowers grow in the forest mold.*

moor[1] /mur/ *v.* Put or keep a ship in place by means of chains or ropes.

moor[2] /mur/ *n.* Open wasteland, especially if heather grows on it.

moral /môr′əl/ *adj.* **1.** Capable of understanding right and wrong: *A baby is not a moral being.* **2.** Good in character. —*n.* The lesson, or inner meaning, or a fable, story, or event: *"Look before you leap" is the moral of the fable.*

morsel /môr′səl/ *n.* **1.** A small bite; a mouthful. **2.** A bit; a small piece.

mortar /môr′tər/ *n.* A mixture of lime, cement, sand, and water for holding bricks or stones together.

moth /môth/ *n.* A winged insect very much like a butterfly, but flying mostly at night. *pl.* **moths** /môᴛʜz/ *or* /môths/.

mountainous /moun′tən əs/ *adj.* **1.** Covered with mountain ranges. **2.** Huge: *a mountainous wave.*

movement /müv′mənt/ *n.* **1.** Moving. **2.** Change in the place of troops or ships. **3.** In music, the kind of rhythm and speed a piece has: *the movement of a waltz.*

murder /mėr′dər/ *n.* Unlawful, intentional killing of a human being. —*v.* Killing of a human being intentionally.

muscle /mus′əl/ *n.* **1.** The tissue in the bodies of people and animals that can be tightened or loosened to make the body move. **2.** Special bundle of such tissue that moves a particular bone or part of the body: *your arm muscles.*

mushroom /mush′rüm′/ *n.* Small fungus shaped like an umbrella and growing very rapidly. —*v.* Grow rapidly.

muskrat /musk′rat/ *n.* A water animal of North America, like a rat, but larger having webbed hind feet, a glossy coat, and musky smell; water rat.

mustard /mus′tərd/ *n.* **1.** A plant whose seeds have a sharp, hot taste. **2.** A powder or paste made of mustard seeds and used to flavor food.

myth /mith/ *n.* **1.** A legend or story that attempts to account for something in nature. **2.** An invented story.

Nn

napkin /nap′ kin/ *n.* Piece of cloth or paper used at meals to protect the clothing or to wipe the lips or fingers.

nectar /nek′ tər/ *n.* **1.** Sweet liquid found in many flowers. Bees gather nectar and make it into honey. **2.** In mythology, the drink of the Greek gods.

neglect /nə glekt′/ *v.* **1.** Leave uncared for: *Don't neglect the plants.* **2.** Omit: *Don't neglect to feed the cat.* —*n.* **1.** Want of attention to what should be done. **2.** Being neglected.

nephew /nef′ ū/ *n.* Son of one's brother, sister, brother-in-law, or sister-in-law.

nerve /nėrv/ *n.* **1.** Fiber or bundle of fibers connecting the spinal cord or brain with the eyes, ears, muscles, and glands. **2.** Courage.

—ness *suffix* used to form nouns from adjectives. Quality or condition of being ____: *Preparedness* means *the state of being prepared.*

neutral /nü′ trəl/ *adj.* **1.** On neither side in a quarrel or war. **2.** Neither one thing nor another. —*n.* A person or country not taking part in a quarrel or war.

newsstand /nüz′ stand′/ *or* /nūz′ stand′/ *n.* Place where newspapers and magazines are sold.

nickname /nik′ nām′/ *n.* Name added to or used instead of a person's real name.

ninety /nīn′ tē/ *n., adj.* Nine times ten; 90. *pl.* **nineties.**

noble /nō′ bəl/ *adj.* **1.** Fine and good in character. **2.** High and great by birth, rank, or title. **3.** Excellent; splendid; magnificent: *a noble scene.* **nobler, noblest.** —*n.* Person high and great by birth, rank, or title.

nook /núk/ *n.* Cozy little corner; hidden spot; sheltered place.

normal /nôr′ məl/ *adj.* **1.** Regular; usual: *The normal temperature of the body is 98.6 degrees.* **2.** Not diseased or defective.

nostril /nos′ trəl/ *n.* Either of the two openings in the nose.

novel /nov′ əl/ *adj.* Strange; new: *Flying gives some people a novel sensation. His invention was a novel idea.* —*n.* Long story with characters and a plot.

nylon /nī′ lon/ *n.* Strong, elastic, and durable substance used to make clothing, stockings, bristles, etc. —*adj.* Made of nylon.

Oo

objection /əb jek′ shən/ *n.* **1.** Reason or argument against something. **2.** A feeling of disapproval or dislike.

obtain /əb tān′/ *v.* Come to have; get through effort.

occasion /ə kā′ zhən/ *n.* **1.** A particular time: *a happy occasion.* **2.** A special event; celebration. **3.** Cause; reason: *The dog was the occasion of our quarrel.* —*v.* Bring about: *His behavior occasioned much laughter.*

odor /ō′ dər/ *n.* Smell: *the odor of roses.*

oilcan /oil′ kan′/ *n.* **1.** Can for holding oil. **2.** Can with a spout for dispensing oil.

omit /ō mit′/ *v.* **1.** Leave out: *He made spelling mistakes because he omitted letters in words.* **2.** Fail to do; neglect: *She omitted making her bed.* **omitted, omitting.**

operator /op′ ər ā′ tər/ *n.* Person who causes something to run or work: *a telephone operator; the operators of a railroad.*

opponent /ə pō′ nənt/ *n.* Person who is on the other side in a game, fight, or discussion: *She defeated her opponents in the election.*

oppose /ə pōz′/ *v.* Be against; resist; try to hinder. **opposed, opposing.**

oral /ôr′ əl/ *adj.* **1.** Spoken; using speech: *An oral agreement is not enough; we must have a written agreement.* **2.** Of the mouth: *The oral opening in the earthworm is small.*

ordinary /ôrd′ ən er′ ē/ *adj.* **1.** Usual; normal.

/a/ ran /ā/ rain /ã/ care /ä/ car /e/ hen /ē/ he /ėr/ her /i/ in /ī/ ice /o/ not /ō/ no /ô/ off /u/ us /ū/ use /ü/ tool /ú/ took /ou/ cow /oi/ boy /ch/ church /hw/ when /ng/ sing /sh/ ship /ŦH/ this /th/ thin /zh/ vision /ə/ about, taken, pencil, lemon, circus

2. Somewhat below average: *The speaker was ordinary and tiresome.*

ore /ôr/ *n.* Mineral or rock containing enough of a metal or metals to make mining it profitable.

outburst /out′bėrst′/ *n.* Bursting forth: *an outburst of laughter.*

outline /out′līn′/ *n.* **1.** The line that shows the shape of an object: *The outline of Italy suggests a boot.* **2.** A brief plan. —*v.* **1.** Draw the outer line of anything. **2.** Give a plan of. **outlined, outlining.**

outskirts /out′skėrts′/ *n. pl.* Outer parts of a town, district, etc.

oval /ō′vəl/ *adj.* Shaped like an egg or like an ellipse. —*n.* Something having an oval shape.

oyster /oi′stər/ *n.* A kind of shellfish much used as food. Oysters are found in shallow waters along seacoasts. Some oysters that live in tropical waters produce pearls. Pearls are produced when a grain of sand gets inside the oyster's shell and is covered with thin layers of liquid from the oyster's body.

Pp

panel /pan′əl/ *n.* **1.** Strip or surface that is different in some way from what is around it: *The front panel in her skirt was made of lace.* **2.** Group formed for discussion: *A panel of teachers discussed the subject of homework.* **3.** Board containing instruments, controls, or indicators used in operating an automobile, aircraft, and the like. —*v.* Arrange in panels; furnish with panels: *We will panel the walls with wood.*

panic /pan′ik/ *n.* Unreasoning fear; fear causing a person or group of persons to lose control of themselves: *There was a panic when fire broke out in the store.* —*v.* Be affected with panic: *The audience panicked when fire broke out.* **panicked, panicking.**

parcel /pär′səl/ *n.* **1.** Bundle; package: *Her arms were filled with parcels.* **2.** Piece: *a parcel of land.*

pardon /pärd′ən/ *n.* **1.** Forgiveness. **2.** Legal document setting a person free. —*v.* **1.** Forgive. **2.** Set free from punishment. **3.** Excuse.

parlor /pär′lər/ *n.* **1.** Room for receiving guests; sitting room. **2.** A shop.

parsley /pärs′lē/ *n.* Garden plant with divided, fragrant leaves. Parsley is used to flavor food and to trim platters of meat and fish. *pl.* **parsleys.**

pathway /path′wā′/ *n.* Path.

patriotic /pā′trē ot′ik/ *adj.* Having or showing love for one's country.

peal /pēl/ *n.* **1.** The loud ringing of bells. **2.** A loud, long sound: *the peal of thunder.* —*v.* Ring out clearly: *The bells pealed forth their messages of joy.*

peanut /pē′nut′/ *n.* Seed like a nut, used for food and for cooking oil.

peerless /pir′ləs/ *adj.* Without an equal: *a peerless performance of the play.*

pension /pen′shən/ *n.* A regular payment that is not wages. —*v.* Give a pension to: *The army pensioned the soldier after years of loyal service.*

perfume /pėr′fūm/ *n.* **1.** Liquid having the sweet smell of flowers. **2.** Sweet smell: *the perfume of the flowers.* /pər fūm′/ *v.* Fill with a sweet odor. **perfumed, perfuming.**

permit /pėr′mit/ *n.* Written order giving permission. /pər mit′/ *v.* Let; allow. **permitted, permitting.**

person /pėr′sən/ *n.* Man, woman, or child; human being.

perspire /pər spīr′/ *v.* Sweat. **perspired, perspiring.**

phrase /frāz/ *n.* **1.** Combination of words. **2.** Expression often used: *"Call up" is a phrase used for "make a telephone call to."* —*v.* Express in a particular way: *She phrased her answer very carefully.* **phrased, phrasing.**

pierce /pirs/ *v.* **1.** Go into; go through: *A tunnel pierced the mountain.* **2.** Make a hole in: *The nail pierced the tire.* **3.** Force a way through: *A loud cry pierced the air.* **pierced, piercing.**

pillar /pil′ər/ *n.* **1.** Column. **2.** Anything slender and upright like a pillar. **3.** An important support: *a pillar of the community.*

pillow /pil′ ō/ *n.* A bag or case filled with feathers or other soft materials, usually used to support the head during rest or sleep.

pistol /pis′ təl/ *n.* Small, short gun held and fired with one hand.

plastic /plas′ tik/ *n.* Any of various substances that can be molded or shaped when hot and become hard when cooled. —*adj.* **1.** Made of plastic: *a plastic bottle.* **2.** Easily molded or shaped: *Clay, wax, and plaster are plastic substances.*

plateau /pla tō′/ *n.* Plain in the mountains; large, high plain. *pl.* **plateaus** /pla tōz′/.

playground /plā′ ground′/ *n.* Place for outdoor play.

pledge /plej/ *v.* Promise solemnly. **pledged, pledging.** —*n.* **1.** Solemn promise. **2.** Thing given to show favor or love: *The ring was a pledge of his love for the queen.*

plenty /plen′ tē/ *n.* All one needs; a large number or amount: *We need plenty of wood for the fire.* —*adj.* Enough; plentiful: *Six potatoes will be plenty.*

plight /plīt/ *n.* Condition or situation, usually bad: *the terrible plight of flood victims.* *syn.* **predicament; dilemma; trouble.**

pointer /poin′ tər/ *n.* **1.** One that points. **2.** Long, tapering stick used in showing things on a map, chalkboard, etc.

pointless /point′ ləs/ *adj.* **1.** Without a point. **2.** Without force or meaning: *a pointless question.*

poise /poiz/ *n.* Balance: *The young girl has poise of mind and body and never seems embarrassed.* —*v.* Balance: *He was poised on the edge of the diving board.* **poised, poising.**

pole /pōl/ *n.* **1.** The North Pole and the South Pole, which are the ends of the earth's axis. **2.** Either end of a magnet. **3.** A long, slender piece of wood.

poll /pōl/ *n.* **1.** Collection of votes: *We had a poll to decide where to have the picnic.* **2.** Number of votes cast: *There was a light poll because of the rain.* **3.** List of voters. **4.** Sur-

vey of public opinion. —*v.* Take the votes of: *The people were polled for president.*

pollution /pə lü′ shən/ *n.* Uncleanness of water, soil, or air.

porter¹ /pôr′ tər/ *n.* Person hired to carry baggage.

porter² /pôr′ tər/ *n.* **1.** Doorkeeper; gatekeeper. **2.** Janitor.

postpone /pōst pōn′/ *v.* Put off until later: *The baseball game was postponed for a day.* **postponed, postponing.**

poultry /pōl′ trē/ *n. pl.* Hens, geese, ducks, etc.

powerful /pou′ ər fəl/ *adj.* Mighty; strong; having great force.

practice /prak′ təs/ *n.* **1.** Action done many times over for skill. **2.** The usual way; custom. **3.** Business of a doctor or lawyer. —*v.* **1.** Do something again and again in order to learn it. **2.** Do usually: *Practice what you preach.* **3.** Work at or follow as a profession: *practice law or medicine.* **practiced, practicing.**

prairie /prãr′ ē/ *n.* Large area of level or rolling land with grass but few or no trees.

praise /prāz/ *v.* **1.** Speak well of. **2.** Worship in words or song: *praise God.* **praised, praising.** —*n.* Act of saying that a thing or person is good; words that tell the value of a person.

prefer /prē fėr′/ *v.* Like better: *She preferred reading to sewing.* **preferred, preferring.**

prescribe /prē skrīb′/ *v.* **1.** Order; direct: *Good citizens do what the law prescribes.* **2.** Order as medicine or treatment: *The doctor prescribed a complete rest.* **prescribed, prescribing.**

prescription /prē skrip′ shən/ *n.* **1.** Order; direction. **2.** A written direction for preparing and using medicine. **3.** The medicine.

presence /prez′ əns/ *n.* **1.** Fact of being present in a place: *Your presence at the meeting is required.* **2.** Place where a person is: *The messenger was admitted to my presence.* *ant.* **absence.**

preserve /prē zėrv′/ *v.* **1.** Save; keep safe. **2.** Keep up; maintain. **3.** Prepare food to keep it

---

/a/ ran /ā/ rain /ã/ care /ä/ car /e/ hen /ē/ he /ėr/ her /i/ in /ī/ ice /o/ not /ō/ no /ô/ off /u/ us
/ū/ use /ů/ tool /ủ/ took /ou/ cow /oi/ boy /ch/ church /hw/ when /ng/ sing /sh/ ship /ŦH/ this
/th/ thin /zh/ vision /ə/ about, taken, pencil, lemon, circus

from spoiling. **preserved, preserving.** —*n.* Place where wild animals and fish are protected. **preserves** /prə zėrvz′/ *n. pl.* Fruit cooked with sugar and sealed from the air.

pretend /prē tend′/ *v.* **1.** Make believe. **2.** Claim. **3.** Claim falsely.

prevention /prə ven′ shən/ *n.* Preventing; hindering: *the prevention of fire.*

preview /prē′ vū′/ *n.* Previous view or inspection; advance showing. —*v.* View beforehand: *We previewed the movie before it was shown to the public.*

previous /prē′ vē əs/ *adj.* Coming before; earlier: *He made a better grade on a previous test.*

prison /priz′ ən/ *n.* Public building in which criminals are confined.

problem /prob′ ləm/ *n.* **1.** Question, especially a difficult question. **2.** A matter of doubt or difficulty. **3.** Something to be worked out: *an arithmetic problem.*

proceed /prō sēd′/ *v.* **1.** Move forward. **2.** Carry on any activity: *proceed to open the door.*

procession /prə sesh′ ən/ *n.* Something that moves forward; persons marching: *A funeral procession filled the street.*

proclaim /prō klām′/ *v.* Make known publicly and officially.

profit /prof′ ət/ *n.* **1.** Gain from a business. **2.** Advantage: *What is the profit in worrying?* —*v.* **1.** Get advantage; gain. **2.** Make a gain in business.

prominent /prom′ ə nənt/ *adj.* **1.** Well-known; important: *a prominent person.* **2.** Easily seen: *The tree in the field is quite prominent.* **3.** Standing out: *prominent eyes.*

promote /prō mōt′/ *v.* **1.** Raise in rank or importance: *The pupils were promoted to a higher grade.* **2.** Start; help to organize: *promote a new company.* **promoted, promoting.**

proof /prüf/ *n.* **1.** Way or means of showing the truth of something: *I have proof of my story.* **2.** Act of testing.

prophet /prof′ ət/ *n.* **1.** Person who tells what will happen. **2.** Person who preaches what he thinks has been revealed to him.

propose /prō pōz′/ *v.* **1.** Put forward for consideration. **2.** Present the name of someone for office or membership. **3.** Intend; plan. **4.** Make an offer of marriage. **proposed, proposing.**

pry[1] /prī/ *v.* Look with curiosity; peep: *He sometimes pries into other people's affairs.* **pried, prying.**

pry[2] /prī/ *v.* **1.** Raise or move by force: *Pry up the stone with your pickax.* **2.** Get with much effort: *We finally pried the secret out of her.* **pried, prying.**

public /pub′ lik/ *n.* People in general; all the people. —*adj.* **1.** Concerning or belonging to the people as a whole. **2.** Not private.

punch[1] /punch/ *v.* **1.** Hit with the fists. **2.** Pierce a hole in. —*n.* **1.** Quick blow or thrust. **2.** Tool for making holes.

punch[2] /punch/ *n.* Drink made of different liquids, often fruit juices.

puppet /pup′ ət/ *n.* **1.** A small doll, often moved by wires. **2.** Anybody who is not independent, but does what somebody else says.

pursue /pėr sü′/ *v.* **1.** Follow to catch; chase. **2.** Try to get: *to pursue pleasure.* **3.** Keep on with: *to pursue the study of music.* **pursued, pursuing.**

Qq

quail[1] /kwāl/ *n.* Any of various plump game birds, especially the bobwhite. *pl.* **quails** or **quail.**

quail[2] /kwāl/ *v.* Lose courage; shrink back with fear: *The dog quailed at the loud noise.*

quite /kwīt/ *adv.* **1.** Completely; entirely: *I am quite alone.* **2.** Really; truly: *quite a change in the weather.* **3.** Very: *quite hot.*

Rr

radiator /rā′ dē ā′ tər/ *n.* **1.** Device for heating a room, consisting of pipes through which hot water or steam passes. **2.** Device for cooling water: *the radiator of a car.*

radius /rā′ dē əs/ *n.* Any line going straight from the center to the outside of a circle or sphere. *pl.* **radii** or **radiuses.**

reason /rē′ zən/ *n.* **1.** Cause: *Tell me your reason for not coming.* **2.** Power to think things out. **3.** Common sense. —*v.* **1.** Think things out: *a baby cannot reason.* **2.** Consider; argue: *It is hard to reason with an angry person.*

reasonable /rē′ zən ə bəl/ *adj.* **1.** Sensible; not foolish: *You can depend on my mother to act in a reasonable way.* **2.** Fair: *a reasonable request.* **3.** Inexpensive: *a reasonable price.*

rebel /reb′ əl/ *n.* Person who resists or fights against authority: *The rebels fought against the government forces.* —*adj.* Defying the law: *a rebel army.* /rē bel′/ *v.* **1.** Resist or fight against: *The oppressed people rebelled against the wicked ruler.* **2.** Feel dislike for: *They rebelled at having to stay indoors on such a fine day.* **rebelled, rebelling.**

reduce /rē düs′/ *or* /rē dūs′/ *v.* **1.** Make less; make smaller. **2.** Become less in weight. **3.** Bring down: *Misfortune reduced them to begging.* **4.** Change to another form: *If you reduce 3 ft., 6 in. to inches, you have 42 inches.* **reduced, reducing.**

reek /rēk/ *v.* Send out a very bad smell; stink. —*n.* A strong, unpleasant smell: *the reek of garbage.*

reflect /rē flekt′/ *v.* **1.** Throw back (light, heat, sound, etc.): *The sidewalks reflected the heat.* **2.** Give back the image: *A mirror reflects your face.* **3.** Think: *to reflect on your blessings.* **4.** Bring: *His grades reflect credit on his family.*

regardless /rē gärd′ ləs/ *adj.* Careless; without heed: *We will go to the meeting, regardless of the weather.*

rejoice /rē jois′/ *v.* **1.** Be glad: *He rejoiced at our success.* **2.** Make glad: *The people were rejoiced by their victory.* **rejoiced, rejoicing.**

reluctant /rē luk′ tənt/ *adj.* Unwilling; slow to act because of unwillingness: *I am reluctant to go out in cold weather.*

remove /rē müv′/ *v.* **1.** Get rid of; put an end to. **2.** Move from place or position. **removed, removing.**

reptile /rep′ tīl/ *or* /rep′ təl/ *n.* Cold-blooded animal that creeps or crawls. Snakes, turtles, crocodiles, alligators, and lizards are reptiles.

require /rē kwīr′/ *v.* **1.** Need: *We require food to live.* **2.** Demand; order: *The rules require us to be present.* **required, requiring.**

residence /rez′ ə dəns/ *n.* **1.** The place where a person lives. **2.** Period of residing in a place: *He had a residence of ten years in France.*

resist /rē zist′/ *v.* **1.** Act against; oppose: *The team resisted all efforts to discourage them.* **2.** Keep from; withstand: *He couldn't resist laughing.*

resistance /rē zis′ təns/ *n.* **1.** Act of striving against: *The bank clerk showed resistance to the robbers.* **2.** Power to strive against: *She has no resistance to germs and is often ill.*

responsible /rē spon′ sə bəl/ *adj.* **1.** Expected to be accountable for: *The pupils are responsible for their own books.* **2.** Deserving credit or blame: *The rain was responsble for a poor corn crop.* **3.** Trustworthy; dependable; reliable: *A responsible person should be chosen.*

result /rē zult′/ *n.* **1.** What is caused: *The result of his fall was a broken leg.* **2.** Good or useful end: *He got good results from the experiment.* —*v.* Follow: *Sickness may result from overeating.*

revere /rē vir′/ *v.* Honor; respect deeply. **revered, revering.**

rigid /rij′ əd/ *adj.* **1.** Stiff; firm; not bending: *a rigid back.* **2.** Strict; stern: *Grandfather had rigid rules about our table manners.*

riot /rī′ ət/ *n.* Disturbance; confusion: *The police stopped several riots on election eve.* —*v.* Behave in a wild, disorderly way.

rival /rī′ vəl/ *n.* Person who wants and tries to get the same thing as another; foe: *The boys were rivals for the same class office.*

/a/ ran /ā/ rain /ã/ care /ä/ car /e/ hen /ē/ he /ėr/ her /i/ in /ī/ ice /o/ not /ō/ no /ô/ off /u/ us
/ū/ use /ü/ tool /ù/ took /ou/ cow /oi/ boy /ch/ church /hw/ when /ng/ sing /sh/ ship /ŦH/ this
/th/ thin /zh/ vision /ə/ about, taken, pencil, lemon, circus

—adj. Wanting the same thing as another: *rival teams; rival stores.* *—v.* Equal; match: *The sunset rivaled the sunrise in beauty.*

roast /rōst/ *v.* **1.** Cook by dry heat; bake. **2.** Make or become very hot. *—n.* Piece of baked meat. *—adj.* Prepared by roasting: *roast beef.*

rocket /rok′ ət/ *n.* Device consisting of a tube open at one end and filled with an explosive or some other substance that burns very rapidly so as to force the tube upward or forward rapidly.

rooftop /rüf′ top′/ *n.* A roof.

rooster /rüs′ tər/ *n.* Male domestic fowl.

rotate /rō′ tāt/ *v.* **1.** Turn in a circle: *Wheels rotate; the earth rotates.* **2.** Take turns; change in regular order: *to rotate crops in a field.* **rotated, rotating.**

rowboat /rō′ bōt′/ *n.* A boat moved by oars.

rowdy /rou′ dē/ *adj.* Rough; disorderly: *a rowdy person.* **rowdier, rowdiest.** *—n.* A rough, disorderly person: *The rowdies ran across the lawn noisily.* *pl.* **rowdies.**

royal /roi′ əl/ *adj.* **1.** Of kings and queens: *the royal palace.* **2.** From or by a king or queen: *a royal command.* **3.** Splendid; fit for a king or queen: *a royal welcome.*

rumor /rü′ mər/ *n.* News without any proof that it is true; vague, general talk: *I heard the rumor about her trip, but I did not believe it.* *—v.* Tell or spread a rumor.

Ss

sacred /sā′ krəd/ *adj.* **1.** Holy: *A church is a sacred building.* **2.** Connected with religion: *sacred music.* **3.** Worthy of reverence: *the sacred memory of a dead hero.* **4.** Not to be violated or disregarded: *She made a sacred promise.*

safety /sāf′ tē/ *n.* Freedom from harm or danger. *—adj.* Bringing no harm; making harm unlikely: *a safety pin.*

salesman /sālz′ mən/ *n.* Man whose work is selling. *pl.* **salesmen.**

salesmen /sālz′ mən/ *n. pl.* See **salesman.**

salty /sôl′ tē/ *adj.* Tasting of salt. **saltier, saltiest.**

saucepan /sôs′ pan′/ *n.* A metal dish with a handle.

saucer /sô′ sər/ *n.* Dish to set a cup on.

scald /skôld/ *v.* **1.** Burn with hot liquid or steam. **2.** Clean with boiling water: *scald the dishes.* **3.** Heat almost to boiling: *scald milk.* *—n.* Burn caused by hot liquid or steam.

scandal /skan′ dəl/ *n.* **1.** Shameful action that brings disgrace. **2.** Damage to reputation. **3.** Evil gossip; slander.

scarce /skãrs/ *adj.* Hard to get; rare: *Good cooks are scarce.* **scarcer, scarcest.**

scarlet /skär′ lət/ *adj.* Very bright red.

scheme /skēm/ *n.* **1.** A plan; a program of action. **2.** A plot: *a scheme to cheat the government.* **3.** System of connected things, parts, etc.: *a color scheme.* *—v.* Plan; plot: *They schemed to bring jewels into the country without paying duty.* **schemed, scheming.**

scholar /skol′ ər/ *n.* **1.** A learned person: *The professor was a famous Latin scholar.* **2.** Pupil; learner: *Each scholar spends three hours a night doing homework.*

scissors /siz′ ərz/ *n.* Tool or instrument for cutting that has two blades so fastened that they will work toward each other. *pl.* or *sing.*

scrawny /skrô′ nē/ *adj.* Thin and bony; lean: *Turkeys have scrawny necks.* **scrawnier, scrawniest.**

screwdriver /skrü′ drīv′ ər/ *n.* Tool for putting in or taking out screws by turning them.

sculptor /skulp′ tər/ *n.* Person who carves or models figures.

sculpture /skulp′ chər/ *n.* **1.** The art of carving or modeling figures. **2.** Sculptured work: *There are some new sculptures in the museum.* *—v.* Carve or model figures. **sculptured, sculpturing.**

seaport /sē′ pôrt′/ *n.* Port or harbor on the seacoast; city or town with a harbor that ships of the sea can reach.

selfishness /sel′ fish nəs/ *n.* Having too much care for oneself and too little for others.

sergeant /sär′ jənt/ *n.* **1.** Army officer ranking just above a corporal. **2.** A police officer ranking next above an ordinary policeman.

service /sėr′ vəs/ *n.* **1.** Helpful act or acts. **2.** Advantage: *Will this car be of service to you?* **3.** Business or system that supplies something useful or necessary: *train service into the city.* **4.** Religious meeting. **5.** Set of dishes. —*v.* Provide with a service of any kind: *service an automobile.* **serviced, servicing.**

sewer /sü′ ər/ *n.* Underground drain to carry off waste water and refuse.

shampoo /sham pü′/ *n.* Preparation used for washing the hair, a rug, etc. —*v.* Wash (the hair, a rug, etc.). **shampooed, shampooing.**

shear /shir/ *v.* **1.** Cut with scissors or shears. **2.** Cut wool or fleece from: *The farmer sheared his sheep.* **3.** Cut close: *The grass on the hill was sheared.* **sheared** or **shorn, shearing.** [These sound alike: **sheer; shear.**]

shears /shirz/ *n. pl.* **1.** Large scissors. **2.** Any cutting instrument like scissors.

shortstop /shôrt′ stop′/ *n.* Baseball player stationed between second and third base.

shovel /shuv′ əl/ *n.* Tool with a broad scoop, used to lift and throw loose matter: *a snow shovel.* —*v.* **1.** Lift and throw with a shovel: *They shoveled the sand into a cart.* **2.** Make with a shovel: *They shoveled a path through the snow.*

shower /shou′ ər/ *n.* **1.** A short fall of rain. **2.** Anything like a fall of rain: *a shower of sparks from the fireplace.* —*v.* **1.** Rain for a short time. **2.** Wet with a shower; spray.

shrivel /shriv′ əl/ *v.* Dry up; wither; shrink and wrinkle: *The grass shriveled in the hot sun.*

sieve /siv/ *n.* Utensil having holes in the bottom to let liquids and small particles pass through, but not the larger pieces.

simply /sim′ plē/ *adv.* **1.** In a simple manner. **2.** Without much ornament; plainly: *simply dressed.* **3.** Merely; only: *He did not simply cry; he yelled.*

sincere /sin sir′/ *adj.* Genuine; honest; free from pretense or deceit. **sincerer, sincerest.**

single /sing′ gəl/ *adj.* **1.** One and no more; only one. **2.** Without others; alone. **3.** Not married: *a single person.* —*n.* Hit in baseball or softball that allows the batter to reach first base only. —*v.* Make such a hit. **singled, singling.**

sleet /slēt/ *n.* Half-frozen rain. —*v.* Come down in sleet.

slogan /slō′ gən/ *n.* Motto: *"Safety first" is our slogan.*

smear /smir/ *v.* **1.** Cover or stain with something sticky, greasy, or dirty. **2.** Rub or spread oil, grease, or paint. **3.** Receive a mark or stain: *Wet paint smears easily.* **4.** Spoil: *smear a reputation.*

smell /smel/ *n.* **1.** Odor; scent. **2.** Sense of smelling: *Smell is keener in dogs than in people.* —*v.* **1.** Recognize by breathing in through the nose. **2.** Give out an odor: *The garden smells of roses.* **3.** Sniff at: *She picked the rose and smelled it.* **smelled** or **smelt, smelling.**

snarl¹ /snärl/ *v.* **1.** Growl and show the teeth. **2.** Say or express with a snarl. —*n.* Sharp, angry words; sharp, angry growl.

snarl² /snärl/ *n.* Tangle: *snarls in the hair.*

snatch /snach/ *v.* Seize suddenly; grab. —*n.* Small amount; bit: *We heard snatches of the music.*

sneer /snir/ *v.* **1.** Show scorn by words or looks. **2.** Say with scorn or contempt: *"Bah," sneered the man.* —*n.* Look or words showing scorn.

soccer /sok′ ər/ *n.* Game played with a round ball between two teams. The players try to drive the ball into the opposing team's goal by kicking it or striking it with any part of the body except the hands and arms.

soda /sō′ də/ *n.* **1.** Any of several substances containing sodium. **2.** Baking soda; sodium bicarbonate. **3.** Soda water.

solar /sō′ lər/ *adj.* **1.** Of the sun: *a solar eclipse.* **2.** Determined by the sun: *solar time.*

soot /sùt/ *n.* Black substance in the smoke from burning coal, wood, oil, or other fuel.

/a/ ran /ā/ rain /ā/ care /ä/ car /e/ hen /ē/ he /ėr/ her /i/ in /ī/ ice /o/ not /ō/ no /ô/ off /u/ us /ū/ use /ů/ tool /ů/ took /ou/ cow /oi/ boy /ch/ church /hw/ when /ng/ sing /sh/ ship /ŦH/ this /th/ thin /zh/ vision /ə/ about, taken, pencil, lemon, circus

soundproof /sound′ prüf′/ *adj.* Not letting any sound pass through. —*v.* Make soundproof: *The halls at our school were soundproofed last year.*

source /sôrs/ *n.* **1.** Person or place from which anything comes or is obtained. **2.** Beginning of a brook or river; spring.

spacecraft /spās′ kraft′/ *n.* Ship that travels in space. *pl.* **spacecraft** or **spacecrafts.**

spareribs /spãr′ ribz′/ *n. pl.* A cut of pork from the part of the rib where there is not much meat.

spark /spärk/ *n.* **1.** Small bit of fire. **2.** Flash that occurs when electricity jumps across an open space. **3.** Flash; gleam. **4.** A glittering bit: *The moving sparks we saw were fireflies.* —*v.* Send out bits of fire; produce sparks.

sparkle /spär′ kəl/ *v.* **1.** Send out little sparks; shine; glitter. **2.** Be lively. **sparkled, sparkling.** —*n.* **1.** A little spark. **2.** Glitter: *the sparkle of the diamond.*

spearmint /spir′ mint′/ *n.* Herb grown for its oil and used to flavor foods.

splendor /splen′ dər/ *n.* **1.** Great brightness: *The sun set in great splendor.* **2.** Glory; pomp: *The pageant was a scene of splendor.*

sponge /spunj/ *n.* **1.** Water animal with a tough elastic skeleton. **2.** Framework of this animal, used for cleaning, soaking up water, etc. **3.** Similar article made of plastic or rubber. —*v.* **1.** Wipe away with a sponge: *Sponge the mud spots off the car.* **2.** Live at the expense of another in a mean way: *The lazy cousins sponge on their family.* **sponged, sponging.**

sponsor /spon′ sər/ *n.* Person who is responsible for a person or thing: *the sponsor of a law; the sponsor of a student applying for a scholarship.* —*v.* Act as a sponsor for: *My scout troop will sponsor one person for summer camp.*

sprawl /sprôl/ *v.* **1.** Lie or sit with the limbs spread out, especially ungracefully. **2.** Spread out in an awkward or irregular manner.

sprout /sprout/ *n.* Shoot of a plant. —*v.* Begin to grow; shoot forth: *Seeds sprout.*

spry /sprī/ *adj.* Lively; nimble. **sprier, spriest** or **spryer, spryest.**

spur /spėr/ *n.* Metal clip with a spike worn on a horseman's heel for urging a horse on. —*v.* **1.** Stick with spurs. **2.** Urge on: *Fame spurred him.* **spurred, spurring.**

squall[1] /skwôl/ *n.* Sudden, violent gust of wind, often with rain, snow, or sleet.

squall[2] /skwôl/ *v.* Cry or scream loudly. —*n.* Loud, harsh cry.

squirt /skwėrt/ *v.* **1.** Force liquid out through a narrow opening. **2.** Come out in a jet or stream. —*n.* The act of squirting: *a squirt of water from the hose.*

stagecoach /stāj′ kōch′/ *n.* Coach carrying passengers and parcels over a regular route.

stairs /stãrz/ *n. pl.* Series of steps going from one level or floor to another.

stairway /stãr′ wā′/ *n.* Stairs; a way up and down by stairs.

stake[1] /stāk/ *n.* Stick or post pointed at one end for driving into the ground. —*v.* **1.** Fasten to a stake or with a stake. **2.** Mark the boundaries of. **staked, staking.**

stake[2] /stāk/ *n.* **1.** Money or thing risked on the result of a game or on any change: *play for high stakes.* **2.** Something to gain or lose; an interest: *Each of us has a stake in the future of our country.* —*v.* Risk something on the result of a game or on any chance: *They staked their money on the black horse.* **staked, staking.**

standby /stand′ bī′/ *n.* Person or thing that can be relied upon either for regular use or for an emergency.

starve /stärv/ *v.* **1.** Die because of hunger; suffer because of hunger. **2.** Feel very hungry. **3.** Weaken or kill with hunger: *The men in the fort were starved into surrendering.* **starved, starving.**

static /stat′ ik/ *adj.* At rest; standing still. —*n.* Electrical disturbance in the air: *Static interferes with radio broadcasting by causing crackling sounds.*

staunch /stônch/ *adj.* **1.** Strong; firm: *staunch walls.* **2.** Loyal: *a staunch friend.* **3.** Watertight: *a staunch boat.*

steak /stāk/ *n.* Slice of meat or fish for cooking. Steak often means beefsteak.

stencil /sten′ səl/ *n.* Device for applying a

pattern, letters, etc., to a surface. Ink or another coloring substance is rubbed over a thin sheet of metal or cardboard into which letters or designs are cut out. —*v.* To make letters or a design by using a stencil.

stick /stik/ *n.* **1.** A long, thin, piece of wood. **2.** Such a piece of wood shaped for a special use: *a hockey stick.* —*v.* **1.** Pierce with a pointed instrument. **2.** Put into a position; place: *Don't stick your head out of the window.* **3.** Fasten; attach: *Stick a stamp on the letter.* **4.** Be at a standstill: *Our car stuck in the mud.* **stuck, sticking.**

stock /stok/ *n.* **1.** Things for use or sale. **2.** Cattle; livestock. **3.** Shares in a company. **4.** Stem or trunk of a tree. —*v.* **1.** Lay in a supply of. **2.** Keep regularly for use or sale: *The store stocks toys at Christmas time.*

stockade /stok ād'/ *n.* A defense or pen made of large, strong posts fixed upright in the ground: *The pioneers built stockades around their cabins to protect them from attack.*

stronghold /strông' hōld'/ *n.* A strong place; safe place; fortress: *The cave was a stronghold for the frightened animal.*

stuck /stuk/ *v.* See **stick.** *We were stuck in the mud.*

stupid /stü' pid/ *or* /stū' pid/ *adj.* **1.** Not intelligent; dull: *a stupid remark.* **2.** Not interesting: *a stupid book.*

sturdy /stėr' dē/ *adj.* Stout; strong; firm: *a sturdy child; a sturdy chair; a sturdy resistance.* **sturdier, sturdiest.**

succeed /sək sēd'/ *v.* **1.** Turn out well. **2.** Come next after; follow: *Adams succeeded Washington as President.*

successful /sək ses' fəl/ *adj.* Prosperous; having success; fortunate: *She was successful in winning the race.*

suffix /suf' iks/ *n.* Word part added to the end of a word to change its meaning or form. *pl.* **suffixes.**

suitable /süt' ə bəl/ *adj.* Fitting; proper; right for the occasion: *a suitable dress for a party.*

sultry /sul' trē/ *adj.* Hot, close, and moist: *We have sultry weather in August.* **sultrier, sultriest.**

sum /sum/ *n.* **1.** The result of adding numbers: *The sum of 3, 2, and 1 is 6.* **2.** Amount of money: *a small sum.*

supreme /sə prēm'/ *or* /sü prēm'/ *adj.* Highest in rank or authority: *a supreme ruler; a supreme court.*

surface /sėr' fəs/ *n.* **1.** The outside of anything: *an egg has a smooth surface.* **2.** Any face or side of a thing: *A cube has six surfaces.* —*v.* Arise to the top of: *The submarine surfaced.* **surfaced, surfacing.**

surfboard /sėrf' bôrd'/ *n.* A long, narrow board for riding the surf.

surplus /sėr' pləs/ *n.* Amount over and above what is needed; excess: *The bank keeps a surplus of money in reserve. pl.* **surpluses.** —*adj.* Extra: *We keep our surplus books in the storeroom.*

surround /sə round'/ *v.* Be around; extend around: *A high fence surrounds the field.*

survive /sər vīv'/ *v.* **1.** Live longer than: *The old man survived his wife by three years.* **2.** Remain: *Those trees have survived for many years.* **survived, surviving.** *syn.* **outlive; outlast; endure.**

swamp /swomp/ *n.* Wet, soft land; marsh. —*v.* **1.** Fill with water and sink: *The waves swamped the boat.* **2.** Overwhelm or be overwhelmed as by a flood: *The factory was swamped with orders.*

sweater /swet' ər/ *n.* A knitted outer garment for the upper part of the body.

swift /swift/ *adj.* **1.** Moving very fast: *swift cars.* **2.** Coming or happening very quickly: *a swift answer.*

system /sis' təm/ *n.* **1.** Set of things or parts forming a whole: *a railroad system.* **2.** An ordered group of facts, beliefs, etc.: *a system of government.* **3.** A plan; a method. **4.** An orderly way of getting things done: *He works by the system.*

/a/ ran /ā/ rain /ã/ care /ä/ car /e/ hen /ē/ he /ėr/ her /i/ in /ī/ ice /o/ not /ō/ no /ô/ off /u/ us
/ū/ use /ü/ tool /ù/ took /ou/ cow /oi/ boy /ch/ church /hw/ when /ng/ sing /sh/ ship /ŦH/ this
/th/ thin /zh/ vision /ə/ about, taken, pencil, lemon, circus

Tt

tablet /tab′ lət/ *n.* **1.** Number of writing sheets fastened together at the edge. **2.** Small flat piece of medicine: *tablets for a head cold.* **3.** Small, flat stone with an inscription: *The tablet tells what historic event took place here.*

tackle /tak′ əl/ *n.* **1.** Equipment; apparatus; gear: *fishing tackle.* **2.** Ropes and pulleys for lifting, lowering, or moving. —*v.* **1.** Try to deal with: *She had several problems to tackle.* **2.** Seize: *John tackled the boy and pulled him to the ground.* **tackled, tackling.**

tantrum /tan′ trəm/ *n.* Fit of bad temper.

tardy /tär′ dē/ *adj.* **1.** Behind time; late: *They were tardy for school.* **2.** Slow: *The bus was tardier than usual.* **tardier, tardiest.**

target /tär′gət/ *n.* **1.** A mark for shooting at. **2.** An object of criticism: *His strange ideas made him the target of jokes.*

teammate /tēm′ māt′/ *n.* A fellow member of a team.

tenant /ten′ ənt/ *n.* Person paying rent for the use of land or buildings: *The apartment has room for one hundred tenants.*

term /tėrm/ *n.* **1.** Word or group of words used in connection with a certain subject: *medical terms.* **2.** Period of time. **3.** One of long periods of time into which a school year is divided. —*v.* Name; call: *The party was termed a success.*

themselves /ᴛʜem selvz′/ *pron.* **1.** Form of *they* or *them* used to make a statement stronger: *The teachers themselves said the test was hard.* **2.** Form used in place of *them* in cases like this: *They hurt themselves sliding downhill.* **3.** Their real selves: *The sick children are not themselves today.*

therefore /ᴛʜãr′ fôr′/ *adv.* For that reason; as a result of that: *She studied hard and therefore passed her test.*

thirst /thėrst/ *n.* **1.** Desire for something to drink. **2.** Dry feeling in the mouth caused by having had nothing to drink. —*v.* Feel thirsty.

thorn /thôrn/ *n.* Sharp point on the stem or branch of a tree or plant.

thrill /thril/ *n.* Shivering, excited feeling. —*v.* Have a shivering, excited feeling.

thumbtack /thum′ tak′/ *n.* Tack with broad, flat head that can be pressed into a surface with the thumb.

tinfoil /tin′ foil′/ *n.* Very thin sheet of tin, or tin and lead, used as a wrapping for candy, tobacco, or similar articles.

title /tī′ təl/ *n.* **1.** The name of a book, song, picture, etc. **2.** A name showing rank, occupation, or position in life. **3.** Championship; first-place position: *He won the golf title.* **4.** Legal right to property; evidence of such a right.

toil /toil/ *n.* Hard work; labor. —*v.* Work hard: *The farmer toiled in the field.*

tongs /tôngz/ *n. pl.* Tool for seizing, holding, or lifting.

tonsil /ton′ səl/ *n.* Either of two small oval masses of tissue on the sides of the throat, just back of the mouth.

toothache /tüth′ āk′/ *n.* Pain in a tooth.

toothbrush /tüth′ brush′/ *n.* Small brush for cleaning the teeth.

topic /top′ ik/ *n.* Subject that people think, talk, or write about: *The topic of the conversation was the hot weather.*

torment /tôr ment′/ *v.* **1.** Cause great pain to: *Headaches torment her.* **2.** Worry or annoy very much: *Flies tormented the horse.* /tôr′ ment/ *n.* A great pain: *A burn can be a torment.*

tough /tuf/ *adj.* **1.** Hard to cut, tear, or chew. **2.** Strong; hardy: *a tough plant.* **3.** Hard; difficult: *tough work.*

tour /tùr/ *v.* **1.** Travel from place to place. **2.** Travel through: *We toured Mexico.* **3.** Walk around: *tour the city.* —*n.* A journey: *a tour of Europe.*

trademark /trād′ märk′/ *n.* Mark, symbol, word, or letters owned and used by a manufacturer or merchant to identify goods.

trash /trash/ *n.* Worthless stuff; rubbish: *Pick up the trash in the yard.*

treacherous /trech′ ər əs/ *adj.* **1.** Not to be trusted; deceitful: *a treacherous enemy.* **2.** Having a false appearance of safety or strength: *Thin ice is treacherous.*

treaty /trē′ tē/ *n.* An agreement between nations. *pl.* **treaties.**

tremble /trem′ bəl/ *v.* **1.** Shake a little; move gently: *The leaves trembled in the breeze.* **2.** Shake because of fear, cold, excitement, etc.; shiver. **trembled, trembling.** —*n.* A trembling: *a tremble in her voice.*

troop /trüp/ *n.* **1.** A group or band of persons: *a troop of boys.* **2.** Herd; flock; swarm. **3.** A unit in the cavalry. **4.** A unit of boy scouts or girl scouts made up of two to four patrols or 16 to 32 members. —*v.* **1.** Move together: *The children trooped around the room.* **2.** Walk; go; go away: *The young girls trooped off after the older ones.*

tropics /trop′ iks/ *n. pl.* Regions near the equator, between 23½ degrees north and south of it: *The hottest parts of the earth are in the tropics.*

trough /trôf/ *n.* **1.** Long, narrow container for holding food or water: *He led his horse to the watering trough.* **2.** Anything shaped like a trough.

trousers /trou′ zərz/ *n. pl.* Two-legged outer garment reaching from the waist to the ankles or knees.

truly /trü′ lē/ *adv.* **1.** In a true manner: *Tell me truly what you think.* **2.** Really: *It was a truly beautiful scene.*

tube /tüb/ *or* /tūb/ *n.* **1.** Long pipe of metal, glass, or other material. **2.** Pipe or tunnel through which something is sent: *The railroad runs under the river in a tube.* **3.** Anything like a tube: *radio tube.*

tulip /tü′ lip/ *or* /tū′ lip/ *n.* A spring flower growing from a bulb and shaped like a cup on a long stem.

tuna /tü′ nə/ *n.* Large sea fish used for food. *pl.* **tuna** *or* **tunas.**

turnstile /tėrn′ stīl′/ *n.* Post with bars that turn, set in an exit or entrance. The bars are turned to let one person through at a time.

typewriter /tīp′ rīt′ ər/ *n.* A machine for making letters on paper.

Uu

unable /un ā′ bəl/ *adj.* Not able.

uneasiness /un ē′ zē nəs/ *n.* Lack of comfort; restlessness; anxiety.

unequal /un ē′ kwəl/ *adj.* **1.** Not the same in size, amount, or value. **2.** Not fair; one-sided: *an unequal contest.*

unite /ū nīt′/ *v.* Join together; make one; join. **united, uniting.**

unlawful /un lô′ fəl/ *adj.* Against the law; illegal; forbidden.

unpleasant /un plez′ ənt/ *adj.* Not pleasant; disagreeable: *unpleasant weather; an unpleasant disposition.*

unselfishness /un sel′ fish nəs/ *n.* More care for others than for oneself; generosity.

unskillful /un skil′ fəl/ *adj.* Awkward; clumsy; not skillful.

untruthful /un trüth′ fəl/ *adj.* Not truthful; contrary to the truth.

unusual /un ū′ zhü əl/ *adj.* Not in common use; not customary.

usual /ū′ zhü əl/ *adj.* In common use; customary; ordinary.

Vv

vain /vān/ *adj.* **1.** Too pleased with oneself; having too much pride in one's looks, ability, etc. **2.** Of no use; unsuccessful.

value /val′ ū/ *n.* **1.** Worth; excellence; importance: *the value of education.* **2.** The real worth; proper price. **3.** Power to buy: *The value of the dollar has gone down.* —*v.* Think highly of; regard highly. **valued, valuing.**

vane /vān/ *n.* Flat piece of metal, or some other device, fixed on a spire or other high object in such a way as to move with the wind and indicate wind direction.

vapor /vā′ pər/ *n.* **1.** Moisture in the air that

/a/ ran /ā/ rain /ã/ care /ä/ car /e/ hen /ē/ he /ėr/ her /i/ in /ī/ ice /o/ not /ō/ no /ô/ off /u/ us /ū/ use /ü/ tool /ù/ took /ou/ cow /oi/ boy /ch/ church /hw/ when /ng/ sing /sh/ ship /ŦH/ this /th/ thin /zh/ vision /ə/ about, taken, pencil, lemon, circus

can be seen; steam from boiling water; fog; mist. **2.** Gas formed from a liquid or solid.

vein /vān/ *n.* **1.** One of the blood vessels that carry blood to the heart. **2.** Rib of a leaf or of an insect's wing.

vessel /ves′ əl/ *n.* **1.** Container; hollow holder. **2.** Ship. **3.** Tube carrying blood or other fluid: *Veins and arteries are blood vessels.*

vibrate /vī′ brāt/ *v.* **1.** Move rapidly to and fro: *A snake's tongue vibrates.* **2.** Quiver. **vibrated, vibrating.**

virus /vī′ rəs/ *n.* Very small substance that causes disease. *pl.* **viruses.**

visible /viz′ ə bəl/ *adj.* **1.** Capable of being seen. **2.** Easily noticed.

void /void/ *n.* An empty space. —*adj.* **1.** Empty; vacant: *a void space.* **2.** Not binding by law: *a void contract.* —*v.* Empty out.

vow /vou/ *n.* Promise. —*v.* Make a solemn promise.

vowel /vou′ əl/ *n.* **1.** An open sound produced by the voice. **2.** Letter that stands for such a sound: *a, e, i, o,* and *u* are vowel letters.

vulgar /vul′ gər/ *adj.* Not refined; coarse: *vulgar words.*

Ww

wallet /wôl′ ət/ *n.* Folding pocketbook.

walnut /wôl′ nut/ *n.* **1.** A rather large nut with a division between the two halves. **2.** The tree this nut grows on. **3.** The wood from this tree.

walrus /wôl′ rəs/ *n.* Large sea animal of the arctic regions, resembling a seal but having long tusks. *pl.* **walruses** or **walrus.**

waltz /wôlts/ *n.* **1.** A smooth, gliding dance. **2.** Music for such a dance. —*v.* **1.** Dance a waltz. **2.** Move nimbly or quickly.

warfare /wär′ fãr′/ *n.* War; fighting.

weakness /wēk′ nəs/ *n.* **1.** Lack of strength, force, power, or vigor: *Weakness kept him in bed.* **2.** Slight fault: *Her weakness is putting things off until later.* **3.** Fondness: *He has a weakness for sweets.*

weary /wir′ ē/ *adj.* **1.** Tired: *weary feet.* **2.** Tiring: *a weary day.* **wearier, weariest.** —*v.* Make or become tired. **wearied, wearying.**

welfare /wel′ fãr′/ *n.* Health, happiness, and prosperity: *the welfare of the family.*

whale /hwāl/ *n.* A mammal that lives in the sea.

whir /hwėr/ *n.* Noise that sounds like whir-r-r: *the whir of machinery.* —*v.* Move quickly with a noise that sounds like whir-r-r: *The motor whirs.* **whirred, whirring.**

whisk /hwisk/ *v.* **1.** Sweep or brush (dust, crumbs, etc.) from a surface. **2.** Move (something) quickly: *She whisked the letter out of sight.* —*n.* **1.** A quick sweep: *a whisk of the broom.* **2.** A light, quick movement.

whoop /hüp/ *n.* Loud cry or shout: *a whoop of rage.* —*v.* Shout loudly: *whoop with joy.*

within /wiṬH in′/ *adv.* **1.** Not beyond; inside the limits of; not more than: *He guessed the weight within ten pounds.* **2.** Inside: *The house was painted within and without.*

wooden /wu̇d′ ən/ *adj.* **1.** Made of wood. **2.** Stiff as wood; awkward: *walked with a wooden gait.* **3.** Dull; stupid: *a wooden speech.*

wooly /wu̇l′ ē/ *adj.* **1.** Consisting of wool: *the wooly coat of a sheep.* **2.** Like wool: *a wooly sweater.* **3.** Covered with wool: *a wooly toy.* **woolier, wooliest.** Also spelled **woolly.**

Yy

yardstick /yärd′ stik′/ *n.* A stick one yard long used for measuring.

yearly /yir′ lē/ *adj.* Coming once a year: *Fourth of July is a yearly holiday.*

yodel /yō′ dəl/ *v.* Sing with frequent changes from the ordinary voice to a shrill voice and back again. **yodeled, yodeling.** —*n.* The act or sound of yodeling.

youngster /yung′ stər/ *n.* **1.** Child: *a lively youngster.* **2.** Young person: *She is as spry as a youngster.*

yuletide or **Yuletide** /ūl′ tīd′/ *n.* Christmas time; Christmas season.